TEN GIRLS WHO USED THEIR TALENTS

LIGHT KEEPERS

Irene Howat

CF4·K

Copyright © 2006 Christian Focus Publications
Reprinted 2007, 2008, 2010, 2012, 2014, 2015, 2016, 2019,
2020, 2022
Paperback ISBN: 978-1-84550-147-1
Epub ISBN: 978-1-84550-856-2
Mobi ISBN: 978-1-84550-857-9

Published by Christian Focus Publications,
Geanies House, Fearn, Tain, Ross-shire,
IV20 1TW, Scotland, Great Britain.
Tel: +44 (0)1862 871011
Fax: +44 (0)1862 871699
www.christianfocus.com
email: info@christianfocus.com
Cover design by Daniel van Straaten
Cover illustration by Elena Temporin,
Milan Illustrations Agency
Printed and bound in China

All incidents retold in these stories are based on true situations.
Where specific information about childhood incidents has been
unobtainable the author has written these paragraphs using other
information concerning family life, hobbies, home life, relationships
freely available in other biographies as well as appropriate historical
source material.

*Cover illustration: This depicts Helen Roseveare waiting for the
train on her way to boarding school. Helen came to love the Lord
Jesus and then went on to do medical work in the Belgian Congo.
Today she travels, writes, teaches, speaks, runs youth groups....*

Dedication
for Gemma and Carol

Contents

Anne Lawson...7

Selina Countess of Huntingdon..........................21

Mildred Cable..35

Katie Ann Mackinnon.....................................49

Sarah Edwards...63

Patricia St John..77

Helen Roseveare...93

Harriet Beecher Stowe..................................107

Mary Verghese..121

Maureen McKenna..137

Quiz...150

Contents

Introduction ....

Midnight Mass of Christmas ....

Midd[illegible] 27

After a[illegible]ination[illegible] 40

Song-[illegible] 61

[illegible] St. John ....

Flash-[illegible] ....

[illegible]eeding 107

Mary [illegible] 121

[illegible] 139

Anne Lawson

Anne Lawson sat on the top bar of the gate and swung her legs. Pip, her corgi dog, lay in the sun beside her. The eight-year-old looked around. East Mains Farm had been her home for as long as she could remember, though she had been born a short distance away in the splendidly named Mains of Machermore. She even knew the colour of the bedroom in which she'd been born. It was pink. But Anne was not a particularly 'pink' girl. Pink made her think of dresses and fluffy things. She was more at home in jeans, and the fluffy things she liked best of all were young animals.

'What do you want to do when you grow up?' visitors to her home asked from time to time.

'Why do people always want to know that?' Anne wondered. 'It's almost as though what you do as a child isn't important, that you've got to be at least fifteen to do anything that matters.'

But Anne knew that wasn't the case. There were always things to be done around the farm, and she knew that she did lots of things that were important in their own way. She especially liked helping her dad, both with his work with the animals, and with any technical things he had to do. If there were loose screws to be tightened, she was there among her dad's tools. If there were rusted nuts and bolts needing oiled to loosen them, she knew fine how to do that too. It was far from unusual for Mr Lawson and Anne to have their heads together under the hood of their Massie Ferguson tractor examining its engine parts.

As she and Pip walked over the field towards the farmhouse, Anne heard a noise that made her legs break into a run. It was the sound of voices. Pip heard them too. Anne had four cousins who stayed on a nearby farm. In fact, the land from one farm led right on to the land of the other. From the fever pitch of laughter that came from the farmyard, Anne knew that all four were in the mood for some fun.

'Just give me a minute to feed the cats,' she yelled to her cousins.

Within two minutes Wee Harry and Arthur had been fed and the fun began.

But when Anne was alone there were two things she especially enjoyed doing. One was reading, and the other was watching the wild creatures that lived in and around the farmyard. Even the books she liked reading were about animals – but prehistoric ones.

'It's Scripture Union day,' Anne thought one morning, as she left for school.

She didn't know why she liked going but she did. It was as though something drew her there.

'You all know about the two Margarets,' the teacher who took S.U. said, 'but it's good to remember their story, especially as they lived so near here.'

Anne listened as her S.U. leader told the story she knew so well, of a teenage girl and an old woman, both called Margaret. They lived at a time in Scottish history when it was not easy to be Christian. If they believed that the Bible said something, and it was different from what the king believed, they could even be killed. The two Margarets were Christians who were tied to stakes in the sands near Wigtown and left there to drown as the tide came in over them. The monument to the two brave Margarets was so well known to young Anne Lawson that she hardly ever noticed it. Nor did she notice the people who visited her part of south-west Scotland. They came to see where the two Margarets and other Christian martyrs had died in the 17th Century because of their faith in Jesus.

When Anne was ten years old, life changed for her. Dad and Mum Lawson sold their farm and moved into a cottage for six months before buying a house in Wigtown. That would have been a big enough change for any girl but, at nearly the same time, Anne went off to boarding school in the Lake District of England.

'I'm going to a group a bit like Scripture Union,' she wrote in a letter some time later. 'Miss Gunning takes it, and it's very good.'

But although she liked and respected Miss Gunning, after a time Anne stopped attending. There seemed to be so much to do as the years passed that there was little time to think about God.

'What do you do at boarding school?' one of her friends from Wigtown Primary School days asked her.

'Work, most of the time,' Anne laughed. 'But you're right, we do loads of other things too.'

'Like what?' the girl asked.

Anne thought about the lunch hours she and her friends spent singing around the school piano, and of her own cello practice, but decided that wasn't what her friend wanted to hear about.

'We go fell-walking,' she said, 'and canoeing and sailing. In fact, we built a canoe last term.'

'It's a shame,' her friend moaned. 'We don't do that kind of thing at school here.'

Anne looked her in the eye. 'Would it really be a good idea?' she asked.

The girl's face creased into a grin. 'Guess not,' she admitted. 'Living in a part of Scotland famous for its treacherous sinking sands would probably not make canoeing the most sensible sport to take up.'

'What are you going to do when you leave school?' her friend asked, as they walked through Wigtown.

It was that question again, but it really was time to think about it seriously now.

'I'm thinking about becoming a vet,' Anne said. 'I've always loved working with animals.'

When Anne did go to university, she went to study zoology. Much of the teaching in her course was based on the theory of evolution, and before long she came to the conclusion that evolution answered all her questions and that God didn't even exist. And that was what she believed when she went for her first job. Anne started work along with four others, two Christians and two who were not. The two Christians, Nash and Kenny, made such an impression on her that she started to read the Bible.

Having done a degree in zoology, Anne discovered that working with dead animals

11

was just what she didn't want to do. She retrained as a metallurgist – someone who understands about metals. After qualifying she looked for a job on an oil rig, but there were no jobs and she found work on land instead.

For eight years Anne searched for the answers to her many questions and she eventually found the answer at a wedding.

'Tell me how you became a Christian,' she was asked, years later. Anne smiled at the memory.

'On 8th July 1989,' she said, 'I went to Kenny's wedding in London. It was the first truly Christian wedding I'd ever been at. Kenny asked me if I was a Christian yet. When I said I was still sitting on the fence, he and his new wife took me into a side room during their own wedding reception, and spoke to me about the Lord Jesus. When I left the room I was a Christian, and I had peace in my heart for the very first time.'

'Would you like to come to a missionary meeting with me?' a member of her church asked Anne, not long afterwards.

Anne Lawson smiled. Her friend seemed to spend her life at missionary meetings.

'Sure, I'll come,' she replied.

'You'll be a missionary one day,' said a lady to the young Christian.

'Yes, I will,' Anne agreed, even though she wasn't quite sure what missionaries really did.

But as she thought back over the years of her life, especially over the last eight years, she realised just how much Jesus had done for her, and told the Lord that she was prepared to be a missionary – or anything else, for that matter – if that's what he wanted.

'Lord, I wish you would show me what you want me to do with my life,' Anne said, as she tidied her writing desk in 1990.

As she spoke aloud to God, she took some leaflets and letters out of the desk. One was a booklet about Mission Aviation Fellowship, and it was appealing for people to serve as aircraft engineers in Tanzania. Anne knew that God had answered her prayer. This was the way forward but what did she have to do first? The following three years were spent training to be both a missionary and an aircraft engineer. And then ... Tanzania!

'We begin the day in the aircraft hangar at Dodoma with worship,' Anne wrote to a friend. 'There is no way I'm going to try to keep aircraft in the air without God's help!'

Then she smiled and settled down to writing a newsy letter.

'You asked what I do, so here we go. Monday was the first day of the Cessna 210

13

OPS 1 check – and I'll explain that to you. OPS (operational) checks are carried out in stages on every aircraft to spread the maintenance. Doing it this way means that aircraft are out of service for short bursts of time on a regular basis rather than being grounded for long periods when they might be needed, and needed urgently.

'Remember,' she went on, 'some of our flights are life saving. The other day a young boy, who had been hurt in an accident, was flown to hospital. The doctor said he would have died before he arrived if he'd gone by road.

'But, back to the maintenance ... the Cessna 206s and 210s have four inspections for every 200 hours of flying. The first one involves a detailed inspection of the fuselage, cabin and landing gear, and a routine inspection of the engine, propeller, wings and tail.'

Anne read over what she'd written and grinned.

'She did ask about my work,' she laughed aloud.

Taking up her pen again, she continued writing.

'The rudder pedals in the cockpit need to be removed for the inspection. And if you think there's no room in a canoe, you've never removed rudder pedals from a Cessna 210. There is space to do it, and space to breath ... lightly. Seriously, getting spanners into some of the spaces is really hard and can take ages. But it needs to be done.'

'I walk miles each day in this hangar,' said Anne to a visitor, after she'd been working there for five years. 'And I'm not just checking aircraft.'

'What else do you do?' the man asked.

'The metal parts of aircraft are not the only things with strengths and weaknesses,' Anne explained. 'All the members of the engineering team have their strengths and weaknesses too. It's up to me as Hangar Foreman to look out for them. Keeping aircraft in the air is a serious business, and everyone involved needs to do their part well.'

'So your job is about people rather than aircraft?' he commented.

'No, it's about both. And it's about housework too.'

The visitor looked puzzled.

'Do you see the size of this huge hangar?' Anne asked. 'Well, it's part of my job to make sure it's kept tidy.'

As they were talking, someone came with a message for Anne.

'Have all the ground checks been done on the Cessna 210?' she was asked.

'Yes,' said Anne, 'and the test flight too.'

'So the aircraft is operational?'

'Yes. Is there an urgent call?'

'A mother giving birth is having problems. Both her life and the baby's life are in danger.'

That was all Anne needed to know. The Cessna 210 was rolled out of the hangar ... and the mother was airlifted to hospital where her baby was born safe and well.

The visitor was still there when, several days later, the aircraft flew to the hospital to pick up the mother and take her home with her new baby.

'That must make all your hard work worthwhile,' he commented to Anne.

'Yes,' she agreed. 'But it's not all about emergency flights. Many of our flights are routine: taking missionaries to remote areas, medical teams to villages, equipment and supplies to hospitals and mission stations and food to areas affected by drought. It's amazing what a day brings.'

Just occasionally, when Anne came back to the UK and spoke about her work, people assumed that she was just an engineer rather than being a missionary herself. They soon learned that things were very different.

'From time to time,' she told them, 'I organize a team of about ten people to go out to villages to encourage the Christians there. After breakfast each morning we have a time of worship. Then we break up and do different things. Some teach new Christians or church leaders, others – and I love doing this – talk to the villagers about the Lord Jesus. Following lunch we have a big outdoor meeting and afterwards we pray for those who are sick. In the evenings we show films in nearby villages using a portable projector and a huge screen. It's exhausting, but great.'

As Anne Lawson sat outside her little home in Dodoma in Tanzania, she looked around and thought of God's care for her. From those distant days at East Mains Farm with Pip at her feet, to Tanzania with Bracken, her Rhodesian Ridgeback dog, God had been with her. Anne returned to Scotland in 2010. She died and went home to heaven six years later.

FACT FILE
Female Aviator
Amy Johnson was one of the world's first female aviators and she flew a Gipsy Moth. She learnt to fly in 1928 at Stag Lane Aerodrome, near Edgware, in the U.K. where de Havilland Moths were built. Unusually she also gained a ground engineer's licence - the first woman in Britain to do this. It was in a Gypsy Moth that Amy made the first solo flight from England to Australia by a woman, in May 1930. She wrote of her 16,000 kilometre (10,000 mile) flight: 'The prospect did not frighten me because I was so appallingly ignorant that I never realised in the least what I had taken on'.

Keynote: Do you think missionary work is glamorous and exciting? Anne maintained planes that saved people's lives. She worked in a different country and met interesting people. However, it is a hard job too. Even missionaries can find some things tedious and tiring. But Anne started the day at the aircraft hangar with worship. Each and every day that we have – be it a good day or a bad day – we should start it off with God. Bring every day to him and ask him to take charge of it.

Think: Anne Lawson prayed one day for God to show her what to do with her life. It is important to pray to God about what he wants us to do. We should ask his opinion about what decisions need to be made. Think about the plans you have for the future – bring them to God first of all. Remember that in the Bible, in Proverbs 16:9, it says that you can make plans in your heart but it is God that is in charge of what actually happens. You may be planning university or college, you may want to get a good job – all these things are fine if that is what God wants you to do. Pray to God to guide you and then do your best at whatever you choose. If you are trusting in God and looking to him for guidance then he will guide your heart and mind to choose the right thing.

 Prayer: Lord God, I have plans for my life but I want these plans to please you. Help me to look to you for guidance. Show me the kind of person you want me to be through your Word. Give me friends who love and trust in you and who will give me good advice. Help me to listen to your Word and to obey it.

Selina, Countess of Huntingdon

'Tell me about Grandfather Shirley,' said Selina. 'It's strange having a grandfather you don't know.'

Sir Robert Shirley looked at his nine-year-old daughter and wondered how much to tell her. Had the time come when she should know more about her family? He decided, with a heavy heart, that it had.

'I think we should go for a walk together,' suggested Sir Robert.

Selina was delighted. She loved her father very much and enjoyed his company.

'Let's go back two generations,' Sir Robert said, as they walked through their land. 'Great-grandfather died a prisoner in the Tower of London. His son, Grandfather Shirley, was born just after he was imprisoned. He married my mother when he was twenty and she was just fifteen. I was the second oldest of eleven children. My older brother died.'

Selina, a very serious-minded girl, listened carefully, remembering every detail.

'My mother died young, and my father married again and more children were born, six of whom are still alive.'

They walked on in silence for a long time. Sir Robert was deep in thought and Selina was trying to work out all she had learned.

'Father,' she said, after a while. 'That still doesn't explain why we don't see Grandfather Shirley. Is it because he's very busy with all his other children?'

Sir Robert shook his head. 'No, I'm afraid not. In fact, your grandfather has fallen out with nearly all the children my mother had. I really don't know how he gets on with the children from his second marriage.'

A weight of sadness seemed to pass from father to daughter as Selina realised exactly why she didn't know her grandfather.

'Father,' said the girl quietly. 'Now that I know these things, will you tell me why Mother left us when I was six years old?'

Sir Robert sighed. 'I can't tell you that, my dear,' he said, 'because I honestly don't know. I suppose your mother expected to be rich and didn't like it that we were not. But after your sister Mary was born she just decided to take the baby and go. They've lived between France and Spain ever since.'

'It's strange not knowing my grandfather,' said Selina, 'but it's even stranger not really knowing my mother and little sister.'

Sir Robert took her hand and they walked together.

'Your mother does keep in touch with you by letter though.'

'Yes, occasionally,' Selina hesitated. 'But they don't really feel as though they come from my mother. They feel as though they've been written by a stranger.'

A few months later Selina saw a very sad thing. A girl about her own age died and she saw the child's body on its way to be buried. She followed the procession and watched all that happened. It made a terrible impression on Selina's young mind and she very often visited the little girl's grave.

'What a serious child Selina is,' a visitor told Sir Robert.

'Yes, I'm afraid that's true. I've done my best for her and her older sister Elizabeth, but they haven't had a normal home life.'

In 1717, when Selina was ten years old, Sir Robert discovered how little he meant to his father. The old man died and, although Sir Robert was the oldest surviving son who should have inherited the family's estates, he was left just £20. Several of his half-brothers and half-sisters were left £5,000.

'I'll fight this through every court in the land,' raged Sir Robert, when he heard the terms of his father's will. How dare he leave an insulting £20 to me, and 250 times that to some of the others. It's a bad business, and the courts can sort it out!'

So began legal battle after legal battle that lasted until after Sir Robert's own death. Selina's father inherited very little from Grandfather Shirley, but she inherited something she would rather not have had – she inherited his very quick temper.

'Everyone is always talking about money,' Selina complained to her sister Elizabeth. 'And it's always about how little they have.'

'But we need money to live on,' said Elizabeth.

'I know that,' agreed Selina, 'but I'm sure there don't need to be all these arguments and court cases. I'm sure we were happier when we lived in Ireland and Father was just a Coldstream Guardsman.'

'Before Mother left home with Mary?'

'That's right,' agreed Selina.

'Look,' said Elizabeth. 'I'm older than you and I can remember things from when you were little, and I can tell you that it wasn't very happy then either.'

Selina then went to her special place to be alone. Tucked away in her special place, she had space to think and pray.

'Please, Lord,' she prayed, 'if you want me to be married one day, please may it be into a serious family.'

Sometimes in her secret place Selina would write letters. Her writing and spelling were awful. Although she grew into a very clever woman, her writing and spelling didn't improve at all.

When Selina married Theophilus, 9th Earl of Huntingdon, in June 1728, she became part of a family with as many problems as her own. But her husband and his half-sisters were different. They were the best of friends. They welcomed Selina into their hearts and she discovered for the very first time what it was like to live in a relaxed and happy home.

Their home, Donnington Park, was welcoming. Many visitors came and went. As Theophilus was not good at business matters, Selina soon knew the estate workers and farmers by name, and all about their families.

'Please make me up a basket of food for the Archer family,' she instructed her cook. 'Mr Archer is ill and his children are hungry.'

'I'll pray for you,' she told people in trouble. And she meant it.

Selina's life was suddenly busy with people she could help and support, and it became busier still when her son was born just a year after she was married.

'Father is hoping to come to Francis's baptism,' she wrote to her sister. 'I'm so looking forward to seeing him.'

But that was not to be. Sir Robert was busy with yet another legal claim involving his wife, then he died quite suddenly just two days before the baptism.

'I'd like to buy Bibles and Prayer Books to distribute when I'm visiting,' Selina told her husband one day.

'What a good idea,' he said. 'You do that.'

Money was no problem now, and Selina was very generous with her wealth. In 1729 she sent £10 to the Society for the Propagation of Christian Knowledge. That was quite a large sum of money then.

Although Selina tried to please the Lord by doing good work, she was not a Christian lady. She had never truly confessed her sins nor asked Jesus to be her Saviour. It was in the late 1730s that she first heard the Bible really being preached, and it wasn't until 1739, when her sister-in-law was converted, that she saw the difference Jesus could make.

'Since I've known and believed in the Lord Jesus Christ for life and salvation, I've been happier than I've ever been,' Lady Margaret enthused.

'Explain to me what you mean,' said Selina.

Lady Margaret did just that, and not long afterwards Selina became a Christian, then Theophilus too.

'This is an exciting time to live,' Selina told her husband. 'Charles and John Wesley, George Whitefield and others are teaching the Bible in a way that's not been done before. No wonder the Church of England won't allow them in their pulpits. We really must do something to help these fine men.'

'What do you suggest?' asked Theophilus. 'Should we help them set up a church?'

'I don't think that's what they want or need,' she replied. 'I think they hope that people's hearts will be changed and that they'll stay in the national church and change it.'

At that time the Church of England was going through difficulties, and the Bible was not being preached as it should have been.

'I think we should help them with money as they don't have a church to provide them with what they need.'

And that's what Theophilus and his wife did. They also attended services held by these keen young men, who were becoming known as Methodists.

'Have you heard about Theophilus and Selina?' one very grand lady said to another. 'They've gone all religious.'

'Really?' questioned her friend. 'They've not joined the Methodists, have they?'

Another woman laughed behind her fan. 'They'll be at prayer meetings next. Talking about religion in public too.'

'It's so unpleasant when people embarrass you by talking about their religion. Some things should be kept strictly private,' complained a sour-faced woman.

'I agree,' said her friend. 'Religion, politics and money should never be discussed in good company.'

A young woman giggled. 'Unless it's someone else's money that's being talked about.'

The woman with the sour face looked so sour that milk might have curdled!

Selina's young sister Mary returned to England and was shocked at her sister's Christian faith. She wrote to Lady Margaret about it. It seems that her writing and spelling were no better than Selina's!

That sect (Methodism) Is so Generally exploded that It's become a Joke of all Compagnys, and Indeed I Can goe no whare but I hear of the uncommon piety of the Donnington family.

What people thought, didn't stop Selina from doing what she believed to be right. Having been brought up comparatively poor, she might have become a mean woman when she became rich. But she did not. She was generous with her money and gave many Bible preachers enough to live on. Even after Theophilus died in 1746 her generosity continued.

'I've been thinking,' she told Lady Margaret. 'Buildings have to be licensed in order to hold official church services in them. The Church of England won't licence buildings for these good men who are preaching today. I wonder if we can do anything about that.'

Lady Margaret shook her head. 'I don't think that even you will manage to change the law, I'm afraid.'

'Perhaps not,' agreed Selina. 'But private chapels are allowed. I think I'll establish private chapels in a number of towns and the Bible can be preached in them.'

'Really, Selina,' laughed Lady Margaret. 'You are full of bright ideas.'

Selina's chapels were built. They were within the law of the land, just. She chose the sites very carefully. All were in towns where the grand people of England went on holiday. She knew that people, who would only go to the Church of England when at home, might try something new on holiday.

'I'm not starting a new church,' she insisted. 'I want people to trust in the Lord Jesus, then go back to the Church of England to spread the good news.'

But that was not how it worked out and Selina was in a way involved in the split.

'What are we going to do?' she asked. 'The students we support are no longer to be accepted for training at Oxford.'

'We could open our own college,' someone suggested.

Immediately Selina was on the case.

'Of course,' she said. 'That's just what we should do.'

That was how Trevecca College in South Wales was started and much of it was paid for by Selina, Countess of Huntingdon.

'The students trained there will be missionaries throughout England,' Selina told her friends. 'Even throughout the world.'

But she was so impatient to see things happen that the young men at Trevecca were sent out preaching so often that for a while they had very little time to study at all. Only as a result of some wise advice in Selina's ear were they given time and peace to get on with their studies.

Trevecca College caused a real problem in the Church of England. Eventually the two groups split and the Countess of Huntingdon's Connexion was formed. There are still some Huntingdon Connexion churches in England today. Just as Selina longed for people to come to the Lord Jesus Christ, those churches today that bear her name still have a strong missionary spirit.

Selina died in 1791.

'What an amazing woman she was,' someone said at her funeral.

'Indeed,' a friend agreed. 'She had such a sad start in life with all her family's rows and ructions. I suppose that's what made her so strong that she was able to do all she did.'

'I'm not as enthusiastic about my religion as Selina was about hers,' said a bystander, 'but I know God changed her life.'

'How do you know that?' he was asked.

The man smiled. 'I knew Selina, Countess of Huntingdon for a very long time. She inherited from her grandfather nothing but his fiery temper. But, after she became a Christian, that temper was tamed. And, if you knew her family, you'd know that only God could tame a Shirley temper.'

FACT FILE
John Wesley
John was born on 17 June 1703 in Epworth, Lincolnshire. He was a renowned preacher and spiritual leader of the 'Methodist revival'. From the 1730s until his death, John Wesley travelled many thousands of miles around Britain on horseback and by carriage, preaching several times each day. He also wrote or edited 400 publications.

Keynote: Selina's family life was very difficult. She barely knew her mother and younger sister. Her grandfather had fallen out with her father too. Family life can indeed be difficult. Selina's family was not happy. Her grandfather was rich but wasn't happy. Her father got married – but he wasn't happy either. His wife left him. Selina was from what we would call a noble family – but without her mother and sister and grandfather her childhood was troubled. Some time later she discovered another family – the family of God. Selina learned that all people are welcome into that family – rich and poor alike. Slaves and noble people are treated the same by our just and merciful God.

Think: Selina's family was famous for having bad tempers. It was said that a bad temper was all that Selina inherited from her grandfather. Think about different things that you have inherited? Perhaps you look or sound like someone in your family? Maybe you have the same name or character? There are lots of things we can 'inherit' from other people. If you have been taught about the Lord Jesus Christ – that is a wonderful inheritance. People have given you the truth from God's word. Ask yourself – 'Do I believe this truth for myself?' You cannot inherit salvation from parents, teachers or anyone else. You must believe in Jesus Christ for yourself. He is the only way to heaven – you can't get there by hitching a ride with another person.

Prayer: Thank you, Lord, for those people in the past who believed and trusted in you. Thank you for the example they left. Thank you for how your Word was taught and how it is still spread around the world today. Help me to trust in you for myself. May I believe in you, and may my family believe in you too.

Mildred Cable

'Where is that girl?' demanded Mrs Cable. 'She moves faster than greased lightening.'

Although she was only seven years old, Mildred Cable was an adventurer. Had the slopes of Mount Everest begun outside her home in Surrey, England, she would have set off to climb it.

'There she is,' her husband laughed. 'Up that tree on the other side of the lane.'

'Which one?' asked Mrs Cable.

'The highest one, of course,' was the answer she expected and the answer she received.

It was Sunday afternoon and the family was out for a walk. But Mildred wasn't looking for a walk - she wanted adventure!

'What would you like to do on the first day of the school holiday?' the child was asked as the end of term drew near. It was 1886.

Mildred grinned. 'I'd like to skate on the frozen River Thames, sledge down the highest hill in England and sail across the Atlantic.'

Mr Cable laughed. 'You need to learn to live in the real world, young lady.'

'What's that?' asked Mildred, a little puzzled. The world that was real to her had no limits because she had such an active imagination.

The reality of Mildred Cable's life was just a little different from what went on in her mind. Her father had a draper's business and, rather than skating on the frozen Thames, sledging down hills and sailing the Atlantic, when she was old enough she found herself sometimes helping her dad at work.

'Could you unpack that box of ribbons?' Mr Cable said, 'and put them in the second drawer from the top.'

Pulling the ribbons between her fingers was lovely. They were pure silk and soft as could be.

'Where do these come from?' she asked.

'That's Chinese silk,' her father replied. 'We sell a lot of Chinese silk ribbon. It's all the fashion just now for threading through white cotton lace.'

But Mildred wasn't listening. The very word Chinese sent her imagination halfway round the world. She was no longer behind the counter of a draper's shop. Instead, she was in a crowded Chinese market, among men with long black pigtails and women dressed in bright-coloured silks.

'For goodness sake, Mildred, you're in a dream.'

Grinning mischievously Mildred proceeded to unpack the ribbons.

'They're just starting to build a Trans-Siberian railway,' she said, 'so you'll maybe be able to buy things from Vladivostok before long.'

Mr Cable shook his head.

'When I was your age I didn't even know Vladivostok existed.'

'It sounds an exciting place, doesn't it?' asked his daughter.

'Mildred,' her mother said in a very serious voice not long afterwards. 'You're a big girl now and you're going to have to start behaving like one. Even your teachers say that you're more interested in adventure than schoolwork. There are plenty of jobs for hard-working young women, but have you ever heard of anyone looking for a female explorer?'

'But I do work at school,' objected Mildred. 'Especially in subjects I like.'

Mr Cable, who was listening to the conversation, realised that geography was one subject his daughter liked. How else would she have known where Vladivostok was? But he decided that he'd best not mention that for fear Mildred told her mother it sounded an exciting place.

'May I go to the mission meeting?' Mildred asked her parents one afternoon.

Her father thought for a moment. 'I don't see why not.'

The meeting in Guildford made a great impression on the girl.

'There's another mission meeting tonight,' she told them the following afternoon. 'May I go to it?'

Mr Cable wasn't quite so keen second time round.

'I don't think so,' he said. 'Anything can happen at meetings like that.'

Mildred couldn't imagine what might happen that her father would worry about. When she didn't appear at the next few mission meetings, her minister decided to speak to Mr Cable.

'I'm just not sure about her going,' the draper said firmly.

'Why not let her come to the closing meeting on Sunday afternoon then?' suggested the minister. 'She can't go to any after that because there aren't any more to go to.'

Mr Cable gave in and Mildred, full of excitement, went to the Sunday afternoon mission meeting. And it turned out to be the beginning of a life-long adventure because she trusted the Lord Jesus that day and came home a Christian. From then on Mildred was a changed girl, even her parents had to admit that.

'There's a missionary from the China Inland Mission speaking tonight,' she told her friends in 1893. 'I'm really looking forward to hearing her.'

Mildred listened to what the young woman had to say with great interest, but something kept catching her eye.

'What is she wearing?' she wondered.

Afterwards, she had an opportunity to speak to the missionary.

'Why do you have a Bible text embroidered on to your collar?' asked the astonished teenager.

'I always do that in China,' the woman explained, 'and I don't see any reason not to do it here.'

Mildred took a deep breath. 'It's not exactly fashionable,' she said, rather too honestly. 'In fact, I think it's embarrassing.'

It says a lot for the missionary that the two of them went on talking on good terms.

'I think the Lord wants you in China,' the woman told Mildred, as they left the hall together.

'If I do become a missionary it will be in India,' the girl announced.

The woman stopped and looked at her young companion.

'You must go where the Lord sends you,' she said. 'If you are Christ's, you must be his entirely.'

Within a year of that conversation Mildred felt sure that God was calling her to be a missionary in China. But she still had no intention of having a Bible verse embroidered on to her collar. From school she went to C.I.M.'s Candidate's Department in North London for six months. C.I.M. stands for China Inland Mission. After that she did a course especially tailored to her needs - a mixture of human sciences, medicine and pharmacy. She did not do the long training required to become a doctor. On 25th September 1901, Mildred sailed for China. Her first year was spent learning the language.

'We have decided to send you to Hwochow in Shansi province,' the young woman was told, when she met with her C.I.M. superior. 'You'll travel there with Evangeline French, an experienced missionary.'

When that decision was made, no one could possibly have guessed that Mildred and Evangeline (Eva), along with Eva's young sister Francesca, would become known worldwide as adventuring missionaries. But to start with there was just Mildred and Eva.

'What beautiful flowers,' said Mildred, as they drew near Hwochow. 'The whole valley is covered in them.'

'Yes, and more's the pity,' Eva replied. 'These poppies are grown for the opium trade. And there's more opium[1] in the air of Hwochow than oxygen!'

'Now, these two rooms are for a girls' school,' they were told, as they were shown round their new home. 'You'll have to work hard here in Hwochow. We all do. Our motto is "When the pressure of work is too heavy, then extend the pressure of work."'

Before long Eva and Mildred knew what was meant by 'the pressure of work.' The two rooms were soon crowded with girls eager to learn, and married women also came for month-long courses in the Christian faith.

Very soon it was known that Mildred had some medical training.

'Send the white woman to cure my ladies' toothache,' the Mandarin of Hwochow ordered.

The young missionary had already discovered that whenever she produced her forceps people clamped their mouths shut. So she carried them where they could not be seen and waited until each patient laughed before thrusting them into the open mouth and extracting the offending tooth.

'The mission starts next week,' Eva told the Hwochow women. 'Bring your friends.'

These missions were a sight to be seen. Women arrived by foot, on donkeys and in mule carts.

---

1. Opium: a highly addictive, narcotic drug.

'Look at them,' said some men who were standing on a street corner. 'There must be 300 women there!'

'I've heard that the men in the church are doing the cooking during their conference,' another commented. 'And look,' he said, pointing in the direction of the church. 'They've laid out books for sale.'

'Let's go and see if there are any interesting books we can buy,' his friend suggested.

Each mission lasted for six days, and nearly every hour of each day was full.

For just over twenty years Mildred and Eva worked in Hwochow.

'Do you think we'll be here for the rest of our lives?' asked Eva, who was beginning to feel that might not be the case.

'No,' replied Mildred. 'I think the time may be coming when we should leave Hwochow, though we love it here.'

'That's how I feel,' Eva agreed. 'But we won't make rash decisions. We'll pray until we're quite sure what we're meant to do.'

Only after a whole year of prayer did the two women agree to leave Hwochow. Both felt that the Lord was leading them to North West China. They were led by God to travel the Gobi Desert gossiping the good news about the Lord Jesus Christ as they went, and distributing Bibles and Christian leaflets along the way.

'You mean you're going to settle in a desert village and start a church there?' someone asked.

'No,' said Mildred. 'We mean that our home will be by the side of the road and that our mission station will be the Silk Road through the great Gobi Desert.'

It was at this point that Eva's sister Francesca joined them. The three women became known as The Trio. The Silk Road was given its name because it was the ancient trade route along which silk and other goods were taken from the East to the West.

From Hwochow the Trio set out with their cart and all their belongings in June 1923, and it took them till March the following year to reach where their long trek was to begin, perhaps because they travelled at about three miles an hour.

'The Gobi Desert is the most amazing place,' said Mildred, two years and many miles later, 'quite apart from being a splendid mission field.'

'It's not much of a field really,' laughed Francesca. 'There is sand everywhere.'

Mildred nodded. 'True,' she said. 'At over 1,100 miles across it's a fair sized sandy mission field.'

'It's interesting, people think of deserts as being flat,' added Eva. 'They don't realise that they are mountainous places, and that hundreds of miles upon hundreds of miles look just the same.'

'Which is probably why people are happy to stop and talk to us about the Lord Jesus, and to come to the meetings we arrange. If you were travelling for many miles you'd be glad to stop and speak to someone.'

'And,' said Mildred, 'if you were on a mule cart, you'd be willing to buy a Bible. You could read right through it in the time it takes to travel the Silk Road.'

'What amazes me,' Eva added, 'is how soon people discover that you have a medical training. You seem to attract those who need your help.'

'It's God who leads us to people, and who leads the right people to us,' concluded Francesca.

That was certainly true about a little girl who arrived at their door in 1925 to beg for money. The poor mite could neither hear nor speak, and she had a dog bite on her leg.

'Why did your dog bite my little girl?' a woman yelled the following day, before demanding money from the missionaries.

'Go away,' said the missionaries' cook very firmly. 'You're a wicked woman.'

When Mildred, Eva and Francesca discovered the girl's story, they heartily agreed.

'The child was seven or eight years old, the daughter of a Mongol chief and a peasant girl. She was sold to that woman when she was just weeks old,' Mildred told a friend, some years later. 'But when she discovered the little girl was deaf and unable to speak, she kept her as a slave rather than a daughter, and sent her out begging every day. That's why we adopted Topsy and brought her up as our own.'

'She's like a daughter to you,' her friend said. 'And a very loving one too.'

In 1936 the three women left their work in the Gobi Desert and returned to the United Kingdom. Topsy went with them, of course.

'Have you retired now?' someone asked Mildred, when the four of them had settled in a little house near Shaftesbury in Dorset.

'It doesn't feel like it,' she replied. 'The Bible Society supported us while we were working abroad. Now we're working for the Bible Society as long as we're able. We continue to write our books. Having travelled to so many interesting places, the least we can do is write about it for others.'

Mildred Cable died in 1952. Eva and Francesca French both died eight years later. And Topsy, who led a happy and interesting life, lived on until 1998. The four women who spent their lives together on earth are now together in heaven with their Lord.

FACT FILE
The Gobi Desert
This is a large desert region in Northern China bounded by the Altay Mountains and the steppes of Mongolia on the north, the Tibetan Plateau to the south-west, and the North China Plain to the south-east. The word Gobi means 'very large and dry' in Mongolian. It was part of the great Mongol Empire.

Keynote: Francesca French mentions in the story that 'It's God who leads us to people, and who leads the right people to us.' Think about the people that you know. God might be leading you to someone for a very special reason. Perhaps he wants you to learn about his love for you and he is bringing someone into your life to teach you. Perhaps he wants to use you to bring someone else to trust in Jesus. Think about the people in your life – and pray about them. Show respect to those Christians who are older than you. If you have older people in your life, they are also gifts from God.

46

Think: The missionary lady with the Bible verse sewn into her collar said something to Mildred which is very important. 'You must go where the Lord sends you,' she said. 'If you are Christ's, you must be his entirely.' Remember this as you go about your day. Everything that you do should be done for the glory of God and you can't hold back any part of your life from the Lord Jesus. The way you act with family and friends should show them that you love Jesus. The things you do at school and outside school should be obedient to God. Don't just follow God at home and at church and then forget about his Word during a sports match.

 Prayer: Lord, help me to see that you are my Creator and the only Saviour. May I realise that every good gift comes from you. You have given me so much, including your Son, the Lord Jesus Christ. Touch my heart so that I will want to belong to you entirely.

Katie Ann Mackinnon

Katie sat on the doorstep and pulled off her wellington boot. Her sock followed, then the eight-year-old had a good look at her heel.

'I knew it,' she said. 'I've got a blister. That's a pest!'

But it wasn't so much of a pest that it would stop her doing what she wanted to do. For when Katie put her mind to it, a little blister wouldn't prevent her having her own way. In fact, when Katie Ann Mackinnon put her mind to something, very little would stop her. With her wellington boot pulled on, she went right back to skipping with her sister. That night she had a really sore heel to show for it.

'Why didn't you come in and take off your boots?' Mum asked.

Katie frowned. 'Imagine being in the house on a nice day in winter. It's bad enough being stuck in when the rain comes and thinks we want it to stay. Why is Scotland so wet?'

'Just because it is,' was the only answer her mother could think of.

That night the girl thought about her blister as she lay in bed. She couldn't help herself, because every time she curled up her heel rubbed against the sheet and reminded her.

'I'm not going to let a stupid blister stop me sleeping,' she told herself. And she didn't!

A day or two later, one of Katie's school friends annoyed her.

'You're a ... You're just a ...'

Katie couldn't think what to call the boy who was being such a pest. Finally, in exasperation, she found the perfect word. 'You're a blister!'

The classroom was suddenly silent as everyone waited for the roof to fall down. But the teacher didn't give Katie a row, for she was struggling not to laugh.

'I've known some real blisters in my life,' she thought, 'Katie Ann Mackinnon among them.'

Katie recognised a close shave when she saw one, and it was probably relief that made her more boisterous than usual when she arrived back home. She was hardly in the door when her mother had to speak sharply to her.

'I'm sorry, Mum,' she said. And she meant it, for Katie's heart was soft and she really didn't like getting into trouble.

One of her sisters let the cat out the bag at teatime, telling Dad that she'd been cheeky in the classroom. As Dad was from the 'punish now and ask questions later' generation, Katie had her telling-off before he heard the whole story.

'You're a real wee blister yourself,' he said, when she explained that she'd not sworn at the teacher. But as he went down to the cowshed, Mr Mackinnon smiled to himself. 'That's a good word for a pest. Trust Katie to think of it.'

'It's not fair,' the girl decided in bed that night. 'I get punished whether I try to be good or not. I can't seem to please anyone at all ... ever.'

Most of all, Katie felt she could never please God. She hated listening to the long sermons preached in her church, and she could never keep her mind on the prayers that seemed to last till the week after next.

One day in 1948, in the town of Oban, Katie discovered someone she could please. And the good feeling it gave her made her decide what she wanted to do with her life. She was in hospital having her appendix out. Normally being stuck in hospital would have bored Katie into mischief – for she was just ten years old – but there was a baby in a cot next to her. Katie watched the nurse working with the baby, and did what she could to help Nurse Mackenzie to care for the little boy.

The nurse was the nicest and kindest person Katie could imagine.

'I'll be a nurse one day,' she decided that night, as she struggled to find a comfortable way to lie to stop her stitches hurting. 'And I'll nurse babies.'

Being away from home and in hospital wasn't easy for a little girl, especially when home was on an island and her family couldn't visit her every day. But Nurse Mackenzie made everything all right.

'I'll be just like her,' thought Katie. 'And everyone will like me for a change.'

Lying in her hospital bed, the girl could imagine what life would be like. She'd spend her days in a sparkling white uniform, gliding from bed to bed fixing a pillow here, changing a bandage there. Just her presence in a ward would make her patients feel better. 'Nurse Mackinnon,' she said softly. 'Sister Mackinnon,' she whispered. 'Yes,' she decided. 'That sounds just right.'

It was eight years later when Katie Ann Mackinnon spent her first day on the wards. She'd been at college for two years, then spent six weeks in nursing school. Now, here she was, ready for whatever was waiting for her on the ward. By the end of day one she had decided that the Ward Sister was the biggest blister she had ever encountered, apart from those on her poor tired feet.

'Have you had a good day?' another student nurse asked her.

'If you'd clapped eyes on my Sister you wouldn't ask that question!' snapped Katie. 'I've danced attention on her all day and she thinks I don't deserve the air I breathe.'

The truth was that Katie had loved it. She was a nurse at last. Well, not exactly a nurse ... not for another three years yet.

Katie's life seemed blighted by blisters. If they weren't on her feet and hands from working so hard, they were telling her what to do. She had many good points, did Nurse Mackinnon, but coping with people in authority wasn't one of them.

'Matron wants to see you in her office,' the young woman was told, some time into her training.

Wondering what she'd done this time kept her busy as she walked briskly along the hospital corridor to her interview. When she left the Matron's office her walk was very different. It was more of slow crawl.

'So,' she gasped, as she headed in the direction of her ward, 'I'll get the sack if I don't improve.'

She could hardly believe what was happening to her. Had she not always wanted to be a nurse? Did she not put everything into caring for patients? What was wrong with her? It didn't take Katie long to answer her own questions. It always boiled down to the same thing. She didn't like doing what she was told if she didn't see the point of it. And she especially didn't like doing what she was told if she didn't respect the person who was doing the telling.

There was one student nurse in the Royal Northern Infirmary in Inverness whom Katie respected very much. Her name was Jean. In her heart Katie knew that she wanted to be friends with Jean, but her fellow student was a Christian and that put her off in a big way. To Katie Christianity meant everlasting sermons and endless long prayers. In one word, Christianity was, in her opinion, B-o-r-i-n-g with a capital B. But after a very serious heart-to-heart talk with Jean and her boyfriend, George, who was a doctor in the hospital, Katie discovered that the opposite was the truth. To her total and utter amazement Katie Mackinnon suddenly realised that what the Bible taught was true, Jesus does change lives. That night he changed her. Katie became a Christian.

Life didn't suddenly become easy for Katie but it was certainly different. She didn't get the sack. In fact, she passed her final exams well and went to work as a staff nurse in Greenock, near Glasgow. After a time there she left to train to be a midwife.

'I said I wanted to nurse children,' she thought. 'Now I know that it was God who put it in my heart. But I wonder what he wants me to do with my life.'

There was a time when Katie Mackinnon was only interested in what she wanted to do. As a Christian it was now her heart's desire to please God.

'Serving God is like being a piece in an enormous jigsaw puzzle,' a missionary told her. 'God has planned for each of us a place of our own and nobody else can fill it.'

In May 1971 Katie Ann Mackinnon discovered where she fitted. Accepted by Africa Inland Mission, she flew to Kenya to work as a missionary nurse among the Kipsigis people. Her work was based in Litein Dispensary, a little hospital with nearly fifty beds ... and no resident doctor.

'I have a pain here,' a man said, after standing in the long queue waiting for treatment.

Katie looked where the man pointed, decided what she thought was wrong with him, and gave him medicine to take for a week. Next in the queue was another man ... and another ... and another. The women were right at the end of the queue.

Katie smiled as each new patient smiled at her. Even without much language, the people knew their missionary cared for them. But they knew she cared for their babies best of all. Katie's face lit up each time she held a tiny baby or a squirming toddler. She had no children of her own but she had space in her heart for every child she met.

'This one won't live,' a helper in the dispensary said, looking at the newborn baby whose mother had died.

When Katie first saw Chepkirui she thought of all that could have been done in Scotland for such a small, ill baby. But neither the equipment nor the medicines were available in Litein.

'Give her a tiny amount of warm milk every three hours and keep her warm. Cuddle her to let her know she's wanted,' she told the teenage hospital carer.

On returning after a clinic, she found Chepkirui abandoned and ignored. When she demanded an explanation, Katie discovered that people thought that babies whose mother died should be left to die too. There was no way that the staff could be persuaded to nurse Chepkirui in a way that would save her life.

'I'll take her home and look after her myself,' decided Katie, much to the astonishment of the hospital staff.

Closing her house door behind her, the missionary felt a surge of joy at the prospect of nursing this scrap of a baby to health and wholeness. And that's just what happened. Chepkirui took her feeds, grew, smiled, giggled and loved Katie with all her tiny heart.

After Chepkirui came Kipngeno, a little boy cursed by a witch doctor.

'She won't risk taking him,' the local people said.

They didn't know Katie. Kipngeno joined Chepkirui, and the pair of them gave her many sleepless nights that were followed by busy days working in the dispensary.

'She'll never keep it up,' some said. 'You're being very silly,' added others. 'You're here to be a missionary, not a mother.' Some people even tried to make life more difficult for Katie than it already was, what with juggling her job and the care of her babies.

'They're real blisters,' she thought, ignoring them when she could, and struggling to work with them when they couldn't be ignored.

It wasn't long before tiny premature Kipkoech joined Chepkirui and Kipngeno. 'She's running a baby home,' some folk said, amazed at Katie's love for these children. That's exactly what God led her to do. Missionary Katie Mackinnon, who had objected to authority as a young person, wanted more than anything to do God's will. Bit-by-bit, the Lord showed her that he wanted her to organise care for needy little children in Kenya.

'How many children are you caring for now?' she was asked, when there were more than twenty.

'Enough to appreciate all the help I can get,' she said. 'Are you offering?'

A couple did offer to help. Matthew and Priscilla, themselves Kenyans, took much of the burden of the children's home – which, by then, was recognised as an official centre for the care of needy children.

'Leave Litein!' Katie gasped. Africa Inland Mission had told her to move to Mulango Dispensary, which was more of a slum than a clinic. Katie was not happy. But at that point she didn't know about Philip, John, Mutuo and Musembe, the first four Mulango babies whom she would love as her own, nor about the others who would follow them. She didn't know about the baby home that would one day be built at Kitui. God had still to show Katie what her part was in his Mulango jigsaw.

'Never in my wildest dreams could I have imagined that we'd have eighty children in the Kitui home during a famine, and that 700 people would come here for food to keep them alive till God sent rain again,' she thought in amazement, after a particularly difficult time in Kenya.

Some years in the future, God had another jigsaw into which Katie was to fit. In 1998,

Matthew, Katie, an architect and a quantity surveyor met in her office. They were drawing up plans for a third home for Kenyan children. This time in Mogogosiek.

'How much money do you have?' the architect asked.

'None,' was Katie's reply.

The two visitors could not have been more surprised if she'd handed them all the money they needed with an ice cream on top!

'God will give us the money as we need it,' explained Katie.

The look on the faces of the architect and quantity surveyor said it all.

But God did just that. Money came in as it was required, and the baby home in Mogogosiek was opened in 1999, not one penny in debt! When Katie Ann Mackinnon retired to her native Scotland, she left three children's homes in the care of Matthew and Priscilla. They were part of God's jigsaw too.

FACT FILE
Africa Inland Mission
AIM was founded over 100 years ago when Peter Cameron Scott gathered around him a group of fellow workers. Cameron Scott records that he '... seemed to see a line of mission stations stretching from the coast, on into the mysteries of the Sahara Desert.' The small group that arrived in Mombasa in 1895 made their way inland. It was not long before disease overtook them and before two years had passed, all but one of them had died. Scott himself died of blackwater fever. But all was not lost. The survivor stayed on and before long others joined him. Over the years the work has spread, initially from Kenya out to Tanzania, Congo, Uganda and Central Africa Republic.

Keynote: As a Christian, it was Katie's desire to please God. Pleasing God does not mean that we are rewarded with forgiveness of sins. Jesus loved us while we were still sinners. He loved us so much he died for us. Forgiveness is given to those who ask for it. It's a gift – not a reward.

Think: Katie was asked by AIM to leave Litein. She had been very happy there and didn't really want to go at first. But in the end she discovered that it had been in God's plan for her to leave as God had seen the needs of the people in Mulango. Sometimes we have to do things that we don't really want to do – like move away from home, go somewhere we hadn't planned or do a job we don't really want to do. God has things to teach us during difficult days as well as during good ones. He can send us in directions we don't want to go and, like Jonah in the Bible, we may want to run in the opposite direction. Instead, we should be obedient and trust in God to help us.

Prayer: Thank you, Lord, for providing for all our needs and for providing for the orphans and children in Katie's orphanages. Thank you that there are people around the world like Katie who have followed your example by loving the people that nobody else wanted to love. Thank you, Lord Jesus, for showing your love to sinners by dying for them on the cross.

Sarah Edwards

Sarah sat on the floor in front of her mother for the nightly ritual of hair brushing. As it was Saturday the hairdressing routine was interesting. The child's long hair was separated into eight or ten bunches then each bunch was wrapped in a strip of damp cloth that was tied at the end. The following morning the cloths – which had dried overnight – were unwrapped and Sarah's fine hair fell into long ringlets around her shoulders. The seven-year-old did a twirl. She liked the feel of her ringlets swinging around her head.

'You look like your grandmother,' her mother said.

'Why?' the child asked. 'Does she twirl to make her hair dance?'

Mrs Pierrepont laughed at the thought.

'I suspect that it's a very long time since Grandma did a twirl,' she said. 'But when she was your age, I'm quite sure she did.'

'Tell me about when my grandmothers were young,' Sarah said.

Her mother thought for a moment.

'Both your grandmothers came from important families. One of your great-grandfathers was the first mayor of New York and another was a founder of Connecticut.'

'How did he found Connecticut?' Sarah asked. 'Was it lost?'

For a minute her mother wasn't sure if the child was being serious, but then she saw the twinkle in her eye.

'Our friends at church will think we're lost if we don't get a move on. The service starts in an hour and you're still not properly dressed.'

Getting dressed in 1717 was a long job. First of all Sarah put on her shift. It was made from rectangles of white linen sewn together and it slipped over her head. Next she put on her stays. This amazing garment was made of heavy linen with wooden splints sewn into it to make her sit and stand properly.

'Don't pull my stays so tight that they pinch,' Sarah told her mother.

'Of course not,' Mrs Pierrepont said. 'Though some women wear their stays so tight I just don't know how they can breathe!'

Having pulled the crisscross laces until they were just comfortable, Mother Pierrepont tied the laces together and tucked them into her daughter's stays.

'I like my Sunday gown,' laughed Sarah, as the material tickled her on its way over her head. 'It's blue like cornflowers.'

Before they left for church the girl wrapped herself in her dark blue cloak and put on her wide-brimmed bonnet, tying its ribbons into a bow to the left of her face. That was the fashion of the day.

'Your father would have loved seeing you looking so fine,' Mrs Pierrepont said, as they walked together to the congregational church in New Haven, on the Atlantic Ocean coast of New England.

'Father died half my life ago,' Sarah said sadly. 'I was four when he died, and I'm nearly eight now. But I remember him very well,' she added.

'What do you remember best?' her mother asked.

'I remember him preaching in church and you sitting at the front facing the congregation – just where you sit now. I could see you both together, and I liked that.'

'It's a strange custom in our church that the minister's wife sits at the front during the service rather than looking at the minister.'

'Did your mother and her mother sit in the same kind of high seats?' the child asked, knowing that her grandfather and great-grandfather had also been ministers.

'Yes, I'm sure they did,' was the reply, as they reached the door of the church.

'Now, Sarah, remember to be quiet and pray before the service. We need to prepare our hearts before we can worship God.'

That was no problem for the seven-year-old. Sarah was often very aware that God was near her, even nearer than people in the same room. There were few times in the week she enjoyed more than the minutes before the church service began. She loved to sit quietly thinking about the Lord. When the service began, she joined the congregation singing praise to God, Sarah was as happy as could be.

'Sarah is a most unusual girl,' a friend told Mrs Pierrepont, as they sat side by side sewing. They always sewed in the window seat, for that's where the light was best.

'I know that,' was the quiet answer. 'Even when she was a little child toddling around at our feet, she seemed to have a sense that the Lord was with her. My husband often said he had never known such a child. But perhaps he was biased,' Mrs Pierrepont smiled. 'After all, she was his own little girl and he was well past the normal age of having a baby daughter to admire.'

The friend thought of the Sarah she knew and loved, and agreed with the late Mr Pierrepont. She was indeed a very special little girl.

In 1723, when Sarah was thirteen years old, a minister and college teacher named Jonathan Edwards met her for the first time. Although he was twenty, he was very taken with the girl.

'She is of a wonderful sweetness, calmness, and universal benevolence of mind,' he wrote. 'She will sometimes go about from place to place, singing sweetly, and seems always to be full of joy and pleasure and no one knows for what. She loves to be alone, walking in the fields and groves, and seems to have someone invisible always conversing with her.'

It was quite true. Sarah did like walking alone, and the 'someone invisible' who kept her company was the Lord.

Just four years later Sarah and Jonathan were married. She was seventeen and he was twenty-four. That was on 28th July 1727.

'Tell me all about your family,' said Jonathan. 'I just love to hear you talking.'

Sarah relaxed beside him. 'We're like your family,' she said. 'Both our families came over from England in order to have freedom to worship God as they wished. And my family has done very well. We have kept to our faith and the Lord has blessed us.'

Jonathan thought of the family into which he had married, and agreed.

'That is true,' he said. 'You're the daughter of a minister, who was the son of a minister, who was the son of yet another minister. And now you've gone and married a minister yourself.'

'And where are you going to be minister?' Sarah teased her new husband.

He laughed heartily. 'In Northampton, with my grandfather, who's a minister. And my father's a minister too. What a pedigree!'

'What a privilege,' said Sarah. 'All those generations of our family have served the Lord. May we also serve him with all our hearts.'

Sarah's first Sunday in Northampton followed the local tradition. She attended church wearing her wedding dress, and sat right at the front, facing the congregation, as she had seen her mother do. It was an honour to sit there, but a problem too.

'What would people think if I yawned?' Sarah asked herself. 'Would they decide that I was finding the sermon boring?'

For the first few months the young couple lived with Jonathan's Grandfather Stoddard. Then they moved to their own home, a homestead with land around it and more land some distance away.

Marriage to Jonathan Edwards was interesting, not least because Sarah saw the back of her husband's head more often than she saw his face.

'How many hours a day does he spend in his study?' a visitor asked one day.

'Thirteen or fourteen,' Sarah replied. 'That's why he's up at five o'clock each morning.'

Her friend smiled. 'I expect you snuggle down to sleep for another hour or two.'

'Not at all,' said her hostess. 'We are all up at five a.m. There's so much to do.'

And Sarah's life was certainly busy. Jonathan had worked out a regime of exercise, diet and sleep that allowed him to concentrate during the long hours in his study. Although she had servants to help her, Sarah made it her business to ensure that his routine went as smoothly as possible. She was a wise woman, for God blessed Jonathan's time in his study. He wrote Christian books that are so important that they have never since been out of print, and can still be bought in shops today.

'What's happening in Northampton?' Sarah asked her husband, soon after their daughter Mary's birth in 1734. She was their fourth daughter. 'The people I meet in the town want to talk about Jesus rather than about their children. I've been asked to more women's prayer meetings recently than ever before.'

Jonathan smiled. 'It's an extraordinary time,' he agreed. 'People are becoming

Christians every week. God is pouring out blessings throughout Connecticut.'

Early the following year he was able to say that thirty people were being converted each week. Sometimes those wanting to talk about Jesus actually queued at the Edwards' door. This wonderful time became known as the 'Great Awakening,' and it continued for eight amazing years. But not everyone was pleased, and Jonathan faced opposition that was hard to bear.

In 1742, just as the Great Awakening was drawing to an end, Sarah had an experience she was never to forget.

'Oh, Mr Edwards,' their servant said, when he came back from preaching away from home. 'Mrs Edwards has been taken really poorly. We've even feared for her life.'

Rushing to his wife, Jonathan discovered that it was not quite as the servant had described, though his poor wife was utterly exhausted.

'Tell me all about it,' he said gently.

Sarah described the experience she had gone through. For seventeen days and nights she had been totally overwhelmed by a sense of God's presence. 'And,' she concluded her story, 'I've handed everything over to God – our lives, our deaths, our everything. It's all in his hands.'

Sarah's trust in God was soon tested. By 1744, when their latest daughter was two and baby Jonathan had just been born, a stranger visited them.

'What's happening?' the man asked Jonathan, seeing soldiers in a watchtower in the Edwards' garden.

'As you know France and England are at war and, amazingly, that puts New Englanders in the thick of it. Some French Canadians are paying Indians to attack our English settlements. A number of locals have been scalped.'

Throughout it all, Sarah was able to put her trust in God.

War was not their only problem. In 1747, having nursed a young missionary who then died of tuberculosis, the Edwards' daughter Jerusha died. She was just seventeen years old. Although Jonathan and Sarah grieved for their daughter, still they were able to trust in the God who does all things well. And they continued to do that when baby Elizabeth was born, even though she was a sickly little girl.

There were even difficulties in the church at Northampton. An issue arose that resulted in Jonathan being asked to leave in 1750. Having been brought up in a wealthy family, for the first time Sarah found herself with no income just weeks after their eleventh, and last, baby was born. He was called Pierrepont, his mother's name before she married.

'It seems that our life is to take on a new direction,' Jonathan said, not long afterwards. And it certainly did, as he became a missionary to the native Indians who lived in Stockbridge, about sixty miles West of Northampton, in October 1751.

'What are you doing?' little Elizabeth asked.

Sarah smiled. 'We used to be able to buy paper for Papa to write on, but we don't have enough money now,' she explained. 'So I'm sewing together all the scraps of paper I can find for him to use.'

'But how can they ever become books?' asked Elizabeth.

Sarah smiled. 'They will if that's what God wants,' she said, pulling Elizabeth on to her knee beside her baby brother.

'Why do you think God brought us here?' asked her son Jonathan, who was thirteen years old.

His mother looked at the tall lad. Many of the Edwards family were tall for their age.

'We don't know what God's plans are,' Sarah said. 'But we do know they are good.'

And God's good plan was that he should learn two American Indian languages and become a missionary to the people whose languages he spoke.

Esther Edwards fell in love with Aaron Burr, and they were married in 1752.

'Your father is a remarkable man,' someone said to her, at the wedding.

The bride agreed.

'And my mother is a most remarkable woman,' she added.

'In what way?' Esther was asked.

'God gave Mother the gift of accepting what happens without grumbling, knowing that the Lord always does what is good, even when we can't see what good will come out of it.'

Five years later, Sarah Edwards' gift of accepting God's will was put to the test yet again. The President of New Jersey College died. Jonathan Edwards accepted an invitation to become President and moved to Princeton in advance of Sarah. Smallpox was a problem and Jonathan was inoculated against the disease. The injection caused him to develop smallpox from which he died. Just before he went to heaven, he was heard to thank God for his married life. But Jonathan and Sarah were not to be separated for long. Shortly after her husband's death, Sarah became unwell and died after just five days' illness. Knowing that God always does what is best, she died in peace.

FACT FILE
Connecticut
This is one of the states of the United States of America. Connecticut is New England's second smallest and southernmost state. It is bordered by New York State on the west, Rhode Island on the east, Massachusetts on the north and by Long Island Sound on the south.

Keynote: Sarah Edwards recognized that being brought up in a Christian home was a privilege. Many of her family were Christians, and many of those family members from her past had been believers in Jesus too. She said, 'May we also serve him with all our hearts.' If you belong to a family who love God, ask yourself, 'have I given my life and heart to Jesus?' If your family doesn't love God, ask yourself the same question. We all need to be saved. If you love Jesus and your family doesn't, you can pray to God to save them too. In the future you may have a family of your own and you can teach your own children to worship God and follow Jesus.

Think: Marriage and careers and work are things that people often think about while growing up. They wonder whom they will marry or what job they will do. If you live your life under God's guidance, reading his Word and obeying his instructions, he will guide you in the right path. The choices you make will be right ones and you will honour God with your life. This is the right thing to do. 'In all your ways acknowledge him and he will direct your paths.' Proverbs 3:6

Prayer: Lord and Heavenly Father, help me to teach others about you, even members of my own family. Teach me from your Word so that I may teach the children of the future to obey your Word and trust in you.

Patricia St John

'Please tell me again about when I was born,' said Patricia. It was one of her favourite stories.

Mrs St John laughed. 'You know it so well you could write a book about it.'

The six-year-old grinned.

'Please ....'

'All right then,' her mother agreed. 'Dad and I were missionaries in Brazil. We loved it there, despite our home being aptly nicknamed 'The House of a Thousand Fleas.' However, Dad was asked to set up Bible schools in remote villages, which would have meant a life of travelling. That was why he went back alone and I stayed here in England with your sister and brother.'

'But you've missed out me being born!'

'Oops. Right, in 1919, not long before Dad returned to Brazil alone, he borrowed a pram big enough to take both your sister and brother. He wasn't used to pushing a pram. It ran out of control and Hazel and Farnham were thrown out. They weren't hurt, but I got such a fright that you were born a few hours later.'

Patricia grinned. 'What a start!'

'Write a story about home,' the teacher said. 'Just a few sentences.'

Patricia St John picked up her pencil.

'Home is called Homesdale and it's in Malvern. Great Granny lives there, and Granny and Mum. Then there's my big sister Hazel and my big brother Farnham, and me. Dad is a missionary in Brazil and only lives with us when he comes to England. We laugh a lot in our home.'

Mrs St John laughed very heartily one day when Patricia's younger brother Oliver was about four. Oliver had made a pretend train with three chairs, one in front of the other. When she came home, the train had Oliver on the front chair driving and Great Granny in her nightgown on the second. Both were bumping up and down saying, 'Puff puff, puff puff'.

'Why are there no other children in our church?' Patricia asked. 'Apart from the Stayputs?'

Granny shook her head. 'You mustn't call those dears the Stayputs. They're so good when they come to church when they're here on holiday.'

The girl nodded. 'That's why we call them the Stayputs. Their hats are always straight on and they never move during the service.'

'Unlike you?' suggested Granny.

'I love church, but I need to move sometimes. And I love Sunday afternoons.'

Smiling, Granny agreed that Sunday afternoons were special.

'Mind you, I don't know how your mother finds time to make these wonderful missionary scrapbooks for you to look at on Sundays.'

'I like our Sunday biscuits,' Patricia said. 'I'm sure there's not another family in England that has Sunday biscuits made in the shape of the letters of the alphabet so that the children can make them into Bible verses.'

After a Sunday story about a little Chinese girl who learned the verse 'Fear not, I have redeemed you; I have called you by name; you are mine' (Isaiah 43:2), Patricia prayed a special prayer. Kneeling down beside her bed, she told God, 'My name is Patricia, and if you are really calling me I want to come and be yours.'

'Look!' she shouted in delight the following morning. 'What beautiful flowers!'

Having become God's child the little girl saw, even more clearly than before, what a beautiful world her Lord had made.

In 1926 Mrs St John took her young family to Switzerland for a year.

'I won't understand what anyone says,' said Patricia, as she set off on her first day at school.

'You'll learn French quickly,' her mother assured her. 'And you'll make friends too.'

She was right. All her life Patricia was a noticing person. She noticed little details and was able to remember them. So, many years later when she wrote *Treasures of the Snow*, she was able to remember details from that year in Switzerland.

Although Patricia had asked the Lord to be her Saviour when she was six, and despite being brought up in a loving Christian home, she was not always a happy teenager. Much of the reason was that her love for the Lord had grown cold. One day, after an angry outburst, Patricia stormed to her room. She was in her mid-teens at the time. Picking up an old Bible that she'd rarely read for some years, she opened it.

'Behold, I stand at the door and knock,' she read from Revelation 3:20, 'if any man hear my voice and open the door, I will come in.'

'It was wonderful,' she told her best friend the next day. 'I seemed to see Jesus standing in a storm saying, "If you will ask me in, I will take you where you want to go."'

Patricia wasn't immediately a happy, carefree teenager, but things began to get better as she read her Bible and prayed to her Lord. But there were always some things that could make her smile.

'What's that noise?' a visitor asked one day.

Patricia's mother was on her feet immediately and on her way to the door.

The girl giggled. 'I think we have unwelcome visitors,' she explained. 'We have ducks down at the end of the orchard. If they see our front door open they march up in single file and come in.'

'What do they do then?' she was asked.

'Well, either Mum chases them out again or they march right through the house and go out the back door.' She laughed at the sounds from the hall, 'It's a Mum chasing them day!'

After school Patricia had hoped to study medicine like her older brother. Unfortunately there was a mix-up with her application form that prevented her from going.

'You can work for me,' her aunt, who ran a school, suggested.

'Helping to teach primary children is not exactly what I want to do,' the girl thought. However, she discovered she enjoyed it very much indeed, thought that job was only a stopgap.

'I've been accepted for nursing training,' she told her aunt in 1942. 'I'm starting at St Thomas's Hospital in London next January.

'What a battle-axe,' Patricia thought, after only two days on the ward. 'I'll never be able to please that Sister.'

'Do this quickly! Do that immediately! Do the other thing yesterday!' barked the Sister, all day, every day.

'Oh my poor fingers,' moaned the young nurse. 'One of them's gone septic.'

Not long afterwards some of her toes became septic too.

'What happening to me?' she asked herself. 'I'm falling apart!'

After a spell off work, Matron suggested she might not be cut out for nursing.

In a fit of despair Patricia went for a walk, eventually arriving at the railway station. There at the entrance, in huge black letters, she read the words, 'Jesus said, "Do you not believe that I am able to do this?"'

Standing in front of the large poster for a long time, the young woman thought hard.

'Yes,' she decided. 'I believe you are able.'

Walking back to the hospital she continued her nursing and did well. When she completed her training, Patricia went home and worked for a local doctor before becoming housemother at her aunt's school.

'You know,' she told her friend. 'So many of these children have missionary parents and they don't see them for years at a time.'

'Do you mother them then?'

Patricia smiled. 'Over the winter months I light a fire in the evenings and the children come down in dressing gowns, clutching their teddy bears, and I tell them a story while they're having their cocoa and biscuits.'

That was the beginning of her storytelling. It was then that she wrote *The Tanglewoods' Secret*. She wrote it, first and foremost, for the children at Clarendon School.

In 1949 Patricia packed her cases and went to be with her brother, a doctor in Tangier, Morocco. For the next year she kept house for him and helped in the hospital. Then the time came when the Lord led her to work in a mountain town above Tangier.

'My little house has a wonderful view,' she wrote home. 'I look down on the market place, then over layers of many roofs to the mountains. Mind you, it does have some disadvantages. Yesterday my room flooded again and I came home to find my saucepan bobbing along like a boat in full sail. Time to go – must get on with my language study.'

And that's what kept Patricia busy for her first few months there, that and completing *Treasures of the Snow*.

'Hello,' she said when she opened her door one day.

'I'm hungry. Can I have some bread?'

Patricia looked at the thin little lad on her doorstep.

'Of course, come in and have some.'

The following night he arrived with five or six of his friends. They'd never tasted bread and treacle before, and they loved it.

'Would you like me to tell you a story?' Patricia asked, as they licked their fingers.

They grinned and said they would. She told them about Jesus, the Good Shepherd. Bread and treacle with a story was a recipe that kept the boys coming back. Wherever she went, Patricia reached right to the heart of children, usually through her stories.

'Goodness me,' laughed Patricia, as she unpacked a parcel one day. 'A clockwork mouse!'

It had come from someone who had heard about the children. The boys and girls loved it, and they were not the only ones.

'Thank you for coming,' the missionary said to the ladies who had attended her meeting.

Nobody moved and more women started to appear. Patricia gave another talk and again thanked the women for coming. No one moved. Puzzled, she waited for an explanation.

'We've come to see the mouse,' admitted one of the ladies.

Greatly amused Patricia took out the clockwork mouse, wound it up, and watched as her visitors screamed at its antics.

'That's one way to encourage women to come to meetings,' she thought, when they did eventually go. 'And they heard two talks about Jesus.'

When winter drew on, and children kept coming to her home for stories, Patricia started to write *Star of Light*, based on what she saw around her at that time.

'Would you come and visit the sick people in our village?' she was asked after a while.

'Yes,' replied Patricia, delighted to have the opportunity to help and to talk about the Lord Jesus Christ.

'Now then,' she said to her helper. 'What do we need?"

Patricia went through a list, 'Iron tablets, malt for mums-to-be, eye ointment and worm medicines, sulphur tablets for babies who have sickness and diarrhoea. What else?'

'Do you have the gentian violet for sores?'

'What would I do without you?' Patricia smiled, popping the gentian violet into her bag.

When she was asked to stay overnight in villages there was more storytelling.

Five years after moving to town, the missionary work began to be opposed.

'There have been complaints about your activities,' she was told. 'And I'm afraid we're cancelling your helper's visa.'

Patricia St John was not the only one who was broken-hearted at the thought of leaving the town. She left many sad friends behind, adults as well as children, but they still remembered her stories. However, as she travelled to England for Christmas she thought over her work in Morocco and smiled. As well as teaching and nursing she'd written *Three Go Searching, The Fourth Candle* and *Star of Light.*

When Patricia returned to Morocco, it was to Tangier where Farnham was a doctor.

'You attract young people,' her brother said, when she set up home with seven teenage girls, all of them student nurses.

'What do I do?' she wrote home in answer to a letter. 'I teach the girls, help look after them, and child-mind for Farnham and Janet's six children when I can. As well as that I help at the baby milk clinic, do what I can in the hospital – and tell stories to anyone who will listen. It's a busy life!'

Patricia's life certainly was busy. In 1966 she left Morocco to go to Rwanda in order to research a book on the history of a period of church growth known as the Rwanda Revival. For some years God blessed Rwanda in an amazing way and Patricia was asked to write a book about it. Of course, her time in Rwanda made her long for revival in her beloved Morocco, that Muslim land in which teaching about Jesus was often far from welcome.

'I've always been fascinated by the story of Onesimus in the Bible,' Patricia told a friend.

'Why don't you write about him then?' was the reply.

'I can't,' explained the storyteller. 'I can only write about places I've been to.'

'Then go!'

That was the start of a trip round Bible sites that enabled her to write *Twice Freed*, the story of Onesimus, the runaway slave.

'I can hardly believe that it's ten years since I wrote about Onesimus,' said Patricia to her sister Hazel in 1976. 'Or that I'm back in the Middle East. What a busy city Beirut is.'

She had gone to help Hazel for a few weeks after she'd fractured her hip in a fall.

'You're doing well on those crutches,' Patricia laughed. 'In fact, you're hopping around like a kangaroo. It won't be long until you'll be well enough to wave me goodbye and send me back to England.'

'No doubt you'll put this visit to good use and write a book based on what you've seen.'

Her younger sister laughed. 'You never know.'

She did. It's called *Nothing Else Matters*.

From then until her death in November 1993, Patricia St John was based in England, though she continued to travel from time to time. When she died and went to heaven she met Jesus, whose stories she had known and loved since before she could remember.

FACT FILE
Morocco
Also known as the Kingdom of Morocco it is bordered by the Mediterranean Sea, the Atlantic Ocean, the Western Sahara, and Algeria. Rabat is the capital and Casablanca the most populous city. Central Morocco consists largely of the Atlas Mountains which rise to 4,167 metres. In the south lie the sandy wastes of the Sahara Desert. The vast majority of Moroccans are Muslims of Arab-Berber ancestry. Arabic is the official language, but French, several Berber dialects, and Spanish are also spoken. On the Atlantic coast, where there are extensive plains, olives, citrus fruits, and wine grapes are grown.

Keynote: Patricia read the words of Jesus Christ, 'Do you not believe that I am able to do this?' When you have problems do you bring them to God and ask him for help? Or do you try and muddle through on your own? Jesus tells us not to worry. He reminds us that God loves us and will look after us. God looks after the sparrows and he will look after you and help you with problems big and small.

Think: 'Behold, I stand at the door and knock, if any man hear my voice and open the door, I will come in,' Revelation 3:20. This is the verse that Patricia read and which brought her back to a stronger relationship with Jesus. She imagined that she could see Jesus standing in a storm saying, 'If you will ask me in, I will take you where you want to go.' Have you asked Jesus into your heart? Are you willing to let him take control of your life and to take you not just where you want to go but to where he wants you to go?

Prayer: Lord Jesus, thank you for all the wonderful stories you told in the Bible. Thank you for the teaching and the truth that we read. Your Word is truth. We can trust it completely. Help me to realise that nothing else matters but you, and that you are the only one who can truly save me from sin.

Helen Roseveare

'You have a new baby sister,' the nurse told Helen, when she was nine years old.

Helen knew all about younger sisters as she already had two. She smiled, 'That means Bob is outnumbered by four to one.'

Numbers played a big part in Helen's home because everyone was so good at doing things with them. Mr Roseveare was a mathematician. Bob, her older brother, could do sums in his head that most people could not do on a sheet of paper. Helen was always top of the class in Maths, and in nearly everything else. In fact, if she was not top of the class, she felt empty inside, as though she had let everyone down. Of course, that made her very popular with her teachers, but it didn't make her popular with the other girls in her school in Preston, Lancashire.

Mr Roseveare, who had started his working life teaching mathematics, was by then a school inspector.

'That's why we move house every three years,' he explained to Helen one day. 'It is very hard to be fair about the work done by people you know and like. And it's even harder to be fair about the work done by people you know and dislike.'

'I dislike moving school so often,' Helen replied.

'It's not for much longer,' smiled her father. 'By next year you'll be ready to go to boarding school.'

In 1937, when she was twelve years old, Helen went to a boarding school in the north of Wales.

'It's different from the other schools Father and Mother took me to see,' she thought, looking round her fellow pupils.

One thing made it especially different and really very modern for its day, and that was the summer uniform. Instead of wearing school dresses and hats, the girls wore culottes and different coloured short-sleeved shirts that opened with three or four buttons at the neck. Of course, they didn't call them culottes in those days; they were known as divided skirts.

Helen felt strange, and very much the new girl. However, before very long she had the beginnings of a friendship – with a Maths teacher. Because she loved Maths and did it so well, her teacher remembered her name very quickly. And as she was an excellent teacher the woman enjoyed her excellent pupil. But not everyone did.

'Teacher's pet,' she heard girls whisper from time to time, though she couldn't always pick out who had said it.

'Helen's a natural hockey player,' the gym mistress said, one lunchtime in the staff-room.

'And a natural mathematician,' said the maths teacher.

'But she's a loner,' another teacher pointed out. 'We'll have to keep an eye on her. Girls who are good at too many things sometimes have problems making friends.'

In a way Helen did have a problem. It wasn't that she felt she had been sent away to boarding school out of her parents' way. Not at all. It was just that she didn't feel loved or special. That made her work hard and play hard because winning prizes and winning games made her feel good.

'The First Form prize this year goes to Helen Roseveare,' the Headmistress said, at her first speech day.

'The Second Form prize this year goes to Helen Roseveare,' she announced, at her next speech day.

'The Third Form prize this year goes to Helen Roseveare,' said the Headmistress, the following year.

'Congratulations!' Her father smiled, pleased with her success.

'Well done!' agreed her mother. 'You're a credit to us.'

Helen felt good. She had pleased her parents by working hard and gaining prizes.

The Second World War broke out in 1939. For a couple of years war had seemed a possibility, then a probability. It was still a shock when Neville Chamberlain, the Prime Minister, made his famous radio broadcast announcing that Britain was at war with Germany. It was hoped that war would be over in a few months. But it wasn't.

Just as she went off to boarding school Helen's family moved to Kent, south-east of London. Wartime visits home could be dramatic.

'Come and count the planes,' her youngest sister called one evening, when the British bombers flew overhead on their nightly mission to drop bombs on Germany.

'One, two, three, four .... Twenty-seven, twenty-eight,' they counted them out.

'Hurry! Hurry! Here they come!' yelled her sister, when the first of the planes could be heard in the distance as they returned. 'Twenty-six, twenty-seven, twenty-eight. They're all back safely!' There was a real sense of relief.

But there were nights when a shadow fell over the household. Sometimes a plane didn't come back from the bombing raid. Helen was old enough to know what that meant to a family somewhere in the United Kingdom.

Of course, bombing raids were made in the other direction too, and they also counted German bombers in and out. There were plenty of them to count, for the bombing was fierce and furious at times. Occasionally a plane was shot down nearby. With her sleeves rolled up, Mrs Roseveare set about cleaning up injuries and comforting the young German pilots.

'I don't know how you can do that,' Helen said. 'They're our enemies!'

Mrs Roseveare looked at her oldest daughter and realised that, although she would soon be going off to university, she still had some growing up to do.

'Why have I come here?' Helen asked herself fearfully, as she looked round Room 12a in Clough Hall on her first day at Cambridge University. 'I'll never fit in. I don't know anyone at all.'

Helen looked in the mirror at her strained face and saw a card tucked under the frame.

'If you don't know anyone, and have nowhere to go after supper, come and have coffee in Room no. 8, at 8 pm. Dorothy.'

Relief, fear, excitement and homesickness hit Helen one at a time, and sometimes all together. But a least someone called Dorothy cared.

As the clock struck eight, Helen made her way to Room 8. She knocked, wondering what kind of reception awaited her.

'Can you make a fire?' a kneeling Dorothy asked, from amidst a swirl of smoke.

What a relief! She could make a fire. And no, Dorothy wasn't perfect, didn't know everyone and everything ... at least she didn't know how to make a fire. Dorothy's welcome and friendship helped Helen settle down at university. But what Helen didn't know then was that Dorothy loved the Lord Jesus Christ and longed for her new friend to love him too. Many prayers were prayed for Helen Roseveare.

'I can't go home at Christmas,' Helen told her friends. 'My young sister has mumps.'

'Why don't you come to the house party at Mount Hermon Bible College?' she was asked.

That's just what she did, and that house party changed her life.

'I'm a failure,' Helen wept, at the end of her last full day there. Tears poured on to her pillow as she lay, face down, on her bed. In desperation she prayed for God to show himself to her. Raising her eyes, she saw a Bible verse on the wall. 'Be still, and know that I am God,' she read. Suddenly her heart filled with peace and joy. She was still, and for the very first time Helen knew God.

'Look at Helen,' a fellow student whispered, when she eventually went downstairs again. 'Her face is absolutely shining!'

From that day on Helen's aim was to discover what the Lord wanted her to do with her life, and to do it as best she could.

'I don't need to struggle to please people now,' she realised one day. 'My life's work is to please my Heavenly Father.'

After graduating from university as a doctor, Helen set off for the Belgian Congo (known today as Democratic Republic of Congo) to serve as a medical missionary with World Evangelisation for Christ (W.E.C.).

On Friday 13th February 1953, in London's Liverpool Street Station, a crowd of friends gathered round her. As the time drew near for Helen's train to leave, an accordion played the first line of a well-known song, and those who had come to see her off joined in the words, 'God be with you till we meet again.' The whistle sounded, the railway guard waved his green flag, and Helen watched as her friends faded into the distance, arms still waving until they could no longer be seen at all.

Helen's journey ended as it had begun, with a crowd around her. 'Welcome to Ibambi,' said a red banner strung across trees decorated for the occasion.

Africans and Europeans sang and smiled and laughed all around her.

'Welcome home, dear,' said Jessie Scholes, a senior missionary.

Then Pastor Ngugu spoke on behalf of them all. 'We, the church of Jesus Christ in Congo, and we, her elders, welcome you, our child, into our midst.'

Helen's heart filled with joy. 'Yes, this is my home,' she realised. 'And I'm loved here.'

All her life Helen had struggled to make people love her. Now, in the Belgian Congo, she was welcomed with love before anyone knew her at all.

From her heart of love Helen served the people who lived in Nebobongo in the rain forest. She delivered babies, performed operations (though she'd never done that before she left England!), and cared for all the needs of a needy people. She even helped build a hospital where Congolese people were trained. There didn't seem to be enough hours in the day to do all that needed to be done. Helen's African friends began to call her Mama Luka, and the more people Mama Luka treated the more people wanted to see her. But Helen never forgot that she was there to share the good news that Jesus is Lord.

It was during a prayer time with some orphan children that a very special thing happened. Helen told the boys and girls about a mother who had died leaving a tiny new baby and a two-year-old daughter. 'The baby needs to be kept warm,' she explained, 'and our very last hot water bottle has burst.'

Ruth, a ten-year-old orphan, prayed for God to send a hot-water bottle today, and a dolly for the baby's sister.

'Help,' thought Helen. Not a single parcel had arrived in all the four years she'd been there.

But a parcel did arrive – that very afternoon. The orphans watched it being unpacked – and there was a hot-water bottle. Ruth rushed forward, knowing what else was inside. She was right. At the very bottom of the parcel was a doll for the baby's big sister.

Twelve years after Helen arrived in Congo there was a rebellion in the country (the Simba Rebellion). White people were no longer welcome and some were cruelly treated. Dear Mama Luka was attacked most terribly. But, even as it was happening, she knew God was with her in a very special way. What happened was so awful that many people reading about it in the newspapers back in the United Kingdom thought Helen would come home, find a job as a village doctor, and try to take life easy. God's plans were different.

'As children we moved home nearly every three years,' Helen remembered, when talking to a new friend in 2006, over forty years later. 'I didn't know that he was preparing me to move from place to place and job to job for the rest of my life.'

'I know you were a missionary doctor till the troubles in the Congo,' her friend said. 'But what else have you done?'

Helen sat upright – she always did – and remembered back over the years since the Simba Rebellion.

'After a time at home I went back to the Congo in 1966, to serve the small town of Nyankunde and a rural area the size of France. An American, Dr Becker, took charge of the hospital in Nyankunde, and my job was to build up a training school. Literally.'

'What do you mean?'

Helen smiled. 'All I had was a hillside and a dream. God gave me a dream of a training school: dormitories, classrooms ... everything. We sent a message out by talking drums asking for students – who were more than surprised to discover they had to build their own dormitories and classrooms. But they did. And in 1973, just before I came home, the school at Nyankunde received official Government recognition.'

'You must have felt that was just the right time to retire.'

Helen Roseveare looked at her new friend and smiled. 'I may be eighty, but I've still not retired. Let me tell you a little bit of how I've spent the last thirty and more years. The Lord allowed me to look after my mother, then to spend some time speaking on behalf of my Mission. After that I spent a year going around the country working with the Girl Crusaders' Union. Amazingly, I have found myself speaking to student groups numbering thousands. God has taken me to Europe, America, Australia and the Far East, even to one country I can't name for fear of Christians there being persecuted. And between all of these things I've written a number of books.'

'I'm speechless,' the other woman said.

'And I was nearly speechless just two years ago when, in 2004, I had the opportunity to go back home to my beloved Nebobongo and Nyankunde, and to see those of my friends there who are still alive. One day I'll see the others again, when we're all home in heaven with Jesus.' Dr Helen Roseveare died and went home to Jesus in 2016.

FACT FILE
W.E.C. International
A man with a burning passion to share the Gospel of Jesus Christ with the un-churched founded W.E.C. International. At fifty-two years of age, Charles T. Studd sailed for Africa in January, 1913. He was called a fool and a fanatic, but a great work was established for the Lord around the world. By the year 2005 W.E.C. had more than 1,719 active workers from forty-nine nations serving in seventy-six different countries, among eighty-three unreached people groups. By 2020 the number of workers has now increased to 1800.

Keynote: After Helen was attacked in the rebellion many people thought she would come home for good, but God's plans were different. The Bible tells us that God's plans are different to our plans. Isaiah 55:8 says, '"For my thoughts are not your thoughts, neither are your ways my ways," declares the Lord.'

Think: Helen said, 'All I had was a hillside and a dream. God gave me a dream.' Think about the dreams and hopes you have for the future. Some of these may be just normal dreams that we all have for the future like marriage or college or some such thing. Other dreams may be ones that God doesn't want for us. But there are still other dreams that have been placed in our heart by God. God will accomplish his plans and, if you are trusting in him, your dreams may be his plans. God will never grow tired or weary. Isaiah 40:28 says, 'The Lord is the everlasting God.'

Prayer: Heavenly Father, you are what a father should be. You are loving and gentle and strong. You are just and fair and right. Thank you for your protection. Change my heart from wanting to please myself to longing to please you.

Harriet Beecher Stowe

It was 14th June 1811, and the cries of a new baby were heard throughout the house. Mr Lyman Beecher looked up from his books and smiled.

'It sounds like a fine strong baby,' he thought, as he rose from the chair and went to meet the newest family member.

'God's given you another healthy little girl,' the nurse told him.

'I wish it had been a boy,' grumbled Mr Beecher, before he went in to see his wife and daughter.

There was no shortage of boys in the Beecher family. By the time all the children had been born, Baby Harriet had two sisters and five brothers.

'Now, remember to say your prayers,' Harriet's older brother told her one night, when she was four years old. 'Ma's ill and can't come to say them with you.'

Harriet knelt, as she always did, at the side of her bed. 'God bless Pa and Ma,' she prayed, 'and all my family. Please forgive me for all I've done wrong, for Jesus' sake, Amen.'

'What have you done wrong?' her brother demanded to know. 'I think you should tell God all about the things you've done wrong.'

'No,' said the little girl. 'Ma says God knows what's in our hearts.'

'But Ma's ill and I'm seeing to your prayers. Pa says I'm old enough to do that.'

Harriet was by then curled up between her sheets and pretending to be asleep.

'Please make Ma better,' she prayed, as she tucked her hand under her cheek and nodded off.

The following morning Harriet knew that her Ma wasn't better even before she opened her eyes. Mrs Beecher suffered from tuberculosis, and the little girl could hear her harsh cough right from the other end of the house. She shivered with fear because, even though she was so young, she knew that people sometimes died of tuberculosis.

'Do you think God will make Ma better?' she asked the cat that had slept all night on her bed. 'Or do you think he'll take her to heaven? He took Mrs Baker to heaven, and she coughed just like Ma.'

'Miew,' the cat said, stretching one leg straight up in the air and washing behind it.

'This house is so quiet since my wife died,' thought Mr Beecher, just two weeks later. 'I never thought I'd miss the noise of my wife's terrible cough. But I do. And the children creep around and hardly make a sound.'

There was a knock at his study door.

'Pa,' said Harriet. 'I've written a story.'

Although she was so young, she had learned to read and write by watching the older children being taught.

'Bring it here and read it to me,' said the minister.

Harriet climbed up on the chair beside her father and began to read.

'There was once a mother who loved her children very much,' she read, following the writing with her finger. 'But Jesus loved her too and wanted to take her home to heaven. When she went away all her children were very sad.'

Mr Beecher blew his nose hard.

'Thank you, Harriet,' he said. 'I'll keep that story in a safe place.'

As she closed the study door behind her, he shook his head.

'To think that I wanted a boy rather than that little girl,' he thought. 'Shame on me.'

Two years later Lyman Beecher was away for a while. Harriet, who slept in the nursery with her two little brothers, knew he was due to come home. The noise of a carriage arriving woke them up.

'Why, here's Pa!' she shouted, as she ran into his arms.

From the shadow behind her father a woman's figure appeared. 'And here's Ma!' a cheery voice called out. Then, bending down to speak to each one of them, the new Mrs Beecher said, 'I'm your new mother. And I love little children.'

'Off to bed now,' Mr Beecher insisted.

'But we want to talk to our new Ma,' the children said together.

Mr Beecher looked stern – and he could look very stern. 'Off to bed.'

Without a word the children left the room. Their new stepmother had spoken the truth. She did love children and she made them very happy.

'What a hustle and bustle,' said Harriet in 1826, when she was fourteen years old. 'There's so much stuff to pack.'

The family was moving from Litchfield in Connecticut north-west to Boston, where her father was to be minister in a larger church.

While Mr Beecher could seem stern and was a very serious preacher, there was another side to him only a few people knew.

'Where's Pa?' asked Charles, Harriet's young brother.

'He's down in the cellar playing in his sandpit,' she replied and giggled. 'Who would ever think a grown man would keep a load of sand in his cellar to shovel from one side to the other just to get rid of excess energy.'

Charles laughed. 'And who would think that a man like our father would have parallel bars, rope ladders, and other such things in the back yard to play on.'

'To keep himself fit on,' corrected Harriet. 'We mustn't laugh at Pa.'

As a teenager Harriet had times of sadness and depression. Her sister Catherine once wrote to Mr Beecher showing how concerned she was.

'I have received some letters from Harriet which made me feel uneasy. She says, "I don't know as I am fit for anything, and I have thought that I could wish to die young. You don't know how perfectly wretched I often feel: so useless, so weak. I tried to appear cheerful, and succeeded so well that Papa reproved me for laughing so much."'

By 1830, Harriet wrote an altogether happier letter to her brother Edward.

'I have never been so happy as this summer. I began it with more suffering that I ever before have felt. But there is One whom I daily thank for all that suffering, since I hope that it has brought me at last to rest entirely in him.'

Harriet had come to realise that it was the Lord Jesus Christ that gave real and lasting joy. That same year there was great excitement in the Beecher household.

'Pa says it's all because of the evil of whisky,' one of his younger children said. 'It wouldn't have happened if that silly man hadn't been storing whisky in the basement of the church.'

'But Pa didn't know when the man rented the room that he was going to use it as a whisky store. He certainly never imagined that what was kept in the basement of the church would explode and burn half the building down.'

As Mr Beecher was furious at what had happened, the children dropped the subject like a hot potato when he entered the room.

'Let that be a lesson to you!' he said firmly. 'You've heard me preaching on the dangers of drink. Now you can see yourself how dangerous it is. When that whisky ignited our church was burned. Those who give themselves over to drunkenness will come to a bad end too!'

There was nothing else to be said on the matter.

Two years after the fire the Beecher family was on the move again, this time to Cincinnati, where Harriet's father was appointed President of Lane Theological Seminary. Cincinnati was just over the river from where slaves were still traded. One day, when Harriet arrived home, she was shaking with emotion.

'It was the most ... the most awful thing I've ever seen,' she said quietly, with tears in her eyes. 'I'll never forget the screams of that poor woman who was sold to a different owner from her husband.' She swallowed hard. 'I caught her husband's eye for a moment. He looked as though his heart had been ripped right out.' Harriet wept at the memory of the terrible scene she had witnessed. 'How can human beings buy and sell other human beings?' she asked. 'How can anyone separate a husband and his wife just for money? I will never forget what I saw today.'

And she never did.

Catherine and Harriet were natural teachers; even as little girls they had loved being taught and teaching. It was not a surprise when they decided to teach and to open a school for girls, the Western Female Institute in Cincinnati.

'We need a geography book for the girls and I can't find one I like,' said Catherine. 'We'll just have to write notes ourselves.'

The sisters could be found late at night in their room listing the rivers of America and the goods that were bought and sold in the major ports. Eventually their work turned into a book that was used in many other schools as well.

'You're good at writing,' people told her. 'God's given you a gift.'

Harriet's gift of writing was confirmed shortly afterwards when she won a writing competition in *The Western Monthly Magazine*.

'I can hardly take in that by this time tomorrow I'll be a married woman,' Harriet told her sister in 1836. She was twenty-five years old and about to marry Calvin Ellis Stowe, a professor at her father's seminary.

'You'll be happy, I'm sure,' her sister said. 'But I'm afraid you'll never be wealthy.'

'I don't care,' laughed Harriet, 'so long as we have enough to live on.'

Calvin and Harriet had seven children in the next fourteen years. Harriet wrote stories and essays to earn money because they really were very poor.

'This is a terrible law!' Harriet raged. It was 1850, and her last child had just been born. 'The Fugitive Slave Law says that anyone giving help or shelter to an escaped slave can be sent to prison. Not only that, but those slaves who have already escaped to freedom in the north are to be sent back to the south to slavery again.'

She sat with her head in her hands. Playing in her mind, like a film repeating itself over and over again, she could see the slave couple of long ago being sold to separate owners. She could still hear the screams of the woman as she watched her husband being shackled. And she could still see the wounded eyes of the poor man as his wife was dragged away.

'I'd do anything to get rid of slavery,' she said aloud. 'Anything at all.'

Harriet's heart was tender. All the talk of slavery kept the subject in her mind. Then the poor woman's heart was broken when her baby son, little Samuel, died of cholera.

'The Lord gave and the Lord took away, blessed be the name of the Lord,' the minister said at Samuel's funeral.

Quietly Harriet said her 'Amen.' Amen means 'so let it be,' and Harriet was handing her baby to her Heavenly Father, knowing that everything he does is right.

The time that followed was busy for Harriet, because she had an idea for a serial story.

'I'll pay you $400 for it,' said the Editor of *The National Era*. 'I'll publish it in forty instalments.'

The National Era was an anti-slavery weekly paper and Harriet's story was very anti-slavery.

'Tell me what it's about,' a friend asked Harriet.

'Wait and see,' she said, 'I've not worked out the end yet. But it's about a gentle giant of a slave called Uncle Tom who is sold by his owner and sent away from his wife and family. Uncle Tom's a Christian and I've just reached a point where the Lord uses him to help the daughter of his new owner to accept Jesus as Saviour.'

Harriet sat writing for hours at a time. Sometimes she was so caught up in the story that tears flowed as she wrote. One such day was when she was writing about how Uncle Tom felt when he was sold.

'O, mas'r, when I was sold away from my old woman and the children, I was just a'most broke up. I felt as if there warn't nothin' left; and then the good Lord, he stood by me, and he says, "Fear not, Tom," and he brings light and joy into a poor feller's soul – makes all peace.'

Months later Harriet's friend called again. 'Do you know how the story ends yet?' she asked. 'I read it every week in the paper and I'm just longing to know how it finishes.'

Harriet, who had just completed the story, nodded. 'Yes,' she said. 'Would you like me to read it to you.'

'I would indeed.'

Harriet sighed. 'Uncle Tom never did get back to his wife and children,' she said. 'He died and, when the message reached the man who had sold him apart from his wife, this is how it was told.' She picked up the final page. *'So, when you rejoice in your freedom, think that you owe it to that good old soul, and pay it back in kindness to his wife and children. Think of your freedom every time you see Uncle Tom's Cabin, and let it be a memorial to put you all in mind to follow in his steps, and be as honest and faithful a Christian as he was.'*

Having been serialised in *The National Era*, *Uncle Tom's Cabin* was published as a book. Slavery was an issue that divided America, an issue that divided families and friends. *Uncle Tom's Cabin* caused a sensation and helped many people to decide that buying and selling people was a terrible thing to do.

Some time later Harriet Beecher Stowe met President Abraham Lincoln. 'So, you're the little woman who wrote the book that started this great war,' said the President, when he realised who she was.

And that war, the American Civil War, was to bring about the end of slavery in America.

Harriet Beecher Stowe died in 1896, having written many other books. But only one of them, *Uncle Tom's Cabin*, helped change the world.

FACT FILE
Uncle Tom's Cabin
Published in March 1852, this book sold three thousand copies on its first day. By the end of its first year it had sold three hundred thousand copies. Harriet Stowe was an ardent abolitionist. It was when her family moved to Cincinnati that she gained first-hand knowledge of slavery and The Underground Railroad. The Underground Railroad was a network of clandestine routes by which African slaves in the 19th century United States attempted to escape to free states, or Canada, with the aid of abolitionists. Other routes led to Mexico or overseas. At its height between 30,000 and 100,000 people escaped enslavement via The Underground Railroad.

Keynote: The fictional character Uncle Tom says the words, 'The good Lord, he stood by me.' Many people who suffered under slavery could testify to the fact that God was with them in their troubles, comforting and helping them. God stood by people in the Bible, like Joseph and Daniel. He stands by us today in the same way. We can rely on our faithful God.

Think: Slavery still exists in many countries today. Even though it has been banished from Western nations, slaves are still smuggled into many countries to work illegally. Many people stood up against slavery and injustice in the past. Christians were strong in taking this stand. Those people believed God's Word and obeyed it. God's Word is true and we must stand up for the truth. We must stand up for those people who are suffering injustice. In Isaiah 7:9 it says if you do not stand firm in your faith you will not stand at all. Christians must stand up for the widows and the fatherless, for the poor and the sick and the suffering. It is one thing to say we believe God's Word, but we must show that we believe it by acting on it.

 Prayer: Thank you, God, for the freedom that Christ brings. Thank you that you are our defender and protector. Lord, help Christians to stand up against injustice and to be the hands that help those who suffer.

Mary Verghese

'I think this is the best place in the whole wild world,' said Mary to Muthi, her ayah[2].

The young woman looked round about her.

'You would think that, Mary, because the Verghese compound is very beautiful. But you don't have to go far down the road to see some very ugly things indeed.'

'But I don't want to think about ugly things today,' argued nine-year-old Mary. 'I want you to play games with me among the trees where it's shady. It's so hot in the sun.'

As they walked together through the beautiful acre-and-a-half compound, Mary struggled to think about nice things. She knew that many people around her home were poor. But she wasn't poor, and today was sunny and she didn't want to be reminded about anything sad.

'I planted that mango tree and the chamba tree over there,' the girl told Muthi. 'My father helped me plant it but I watered it all by myself.'

---

2. Ayah - Indian name for nurse or nanny.

'Did he really help you plant these trees?' Muthi asked in surprise. 'I thought he would have one of his servants do that.'

Mary smiled. 'No, he helped me himself. You see, my brothers had already planted trees and mine is in competition with their ones. Father helped me to dig a hole and prepare the soil in order that the trees would root well and catch up with the boys' ones.'

'You have a good father,' Muthi commented. 'Not every little girl in India has such a good father.'

Mary stood under the shade of a plantain tree and looked around.

'Will you play "I spy" with me?' she asked her ayah.

The nursemaid nodded. 'I spy with my little eye something beginning with T.'

It only took Mary one guess to know it was a tamarind tree.

'Again!' she demanded.

'I spy with my little eye something beginning with J.'

'That's the jackfruit,' guessed Mary correctly. 'But it's going to be boring if you only spy trees.'

'OK then,' said Muthi, who was bored with the game anyway. 'I spy with my little eye something beginning with J.'

'We've done the jackfruit,' Mary sulked.

'It's another J.'

Mary looked around with interest, but couldn't see a single thing beginning with J.

'I give up. What is it?'

The ayah was pleased with her success. 'It's Joseph. He's at the gate.'

A shudder went up Mary's back.

'I'm going to play with my doll. That was bad of you to make me guess Joseph.'

Sitting in the veranda of her home, Mary looked as though she was playing with her doll, but she was not. In fact, she was watching and listening, because a very interesting thing was happening at the garden gate.

'Pakavum,' said one of the maids, warning the others of danger.

'Why do they think Joseph is dangerous?' Mary asked her doll.

Then there was her mother's voice. 'Adukkallai!'

'It's all right, Mum,' the girl called. 'I'm not going to go near.'

Mary hugged her doll.

'It's strange,' she said. 'One is shouting "dangerous" and another is shouting "don't go near," while Joseph at the gate is shouting "Praise the Lord!" I wonder why I'm not allowed to go near Joseph. Can it be just because he's so ugly. Perhaps they think I'd be frightened if I saw him close up. But I'm not frightened of ugly things, I just don't like to see them on sunny days.'

The next time she heard Joseph's voice further along the road, Mary hid behind a pile of coconut palm leaves near the gate and waited until someone in the house heard him shouting, 'Praise the Lord.' She did not have very long to wait.

'Here comes Muthi,' she whispered to her doll. 'And the cook has given her a basket of food for Joseph.'

She watched as Muthi came down the path to the gate, walking more slowly as she drew near Joseph, even though there was a wall and a gate between them. Fascinated, Mary stayed out of sight.

'Look,' she whispered. 'Muthi has opened the gate, laid the basket down, and rushed away. Surely Joseph can't be so ugly that my ayah's frightened?'

Suddenly the girl felt as though she had turned to stone. She didn't see much of the beggar's face and hands but she saw enough. Joseph had leprosy! Scared out of her wits, she scrambled right through the scratchy coconut palm leaves and ran into the house.

'Mum! Mum!' she called. 'Don't let Muthi give Joseph any more food. He has leprosy!'

Mrs Verghese settled in a shady part of the veranda and pulled her daughter on to her knee.

'Yes,' she said. 'I know Joseph has leprosy. And now that you are a big girl, I have to explain to you about leprosy because you will soon be old enough to leave the compound without your ayah, and you need to know what to do if you meet someone with leprosy.'

'I'd run away,' said Mary. 'Fast!'

'I want you to listen very carefully to what I have to say,' Mrs Verghese said. 'These poor sad people have a disease that damages them terribly. It eats away at their fingers and toes, sometimes even at parts of their faces.'

Mary turned away from her mother. 'I don't want to know,' she said. 'It's sunny and I don't want to think about ugly things.'

Hugging her daughter close, Mrs Verghese refused to be put off. 'There are many ugly things in life, Mary, and they are there whether the sun shines or not. It's time you realised that.'

The girl knew from her mother's tone of voice that she had lost the battle. She was just going to have to sit and listen to whatever was to be said.

'If you meet someone with leprosy you do not turn and run away. Think how you would feel if you had that terrible disease and everyone ran away from you,' said Mrs Verghese.

'But I could never touch one of them,' the girl whispered.

'Of course not,' her mother said, horrified at the thought. 'But you smile at them then walk on quickly, being very careful not to go near them, and certainly never to touch them.'

Mary Verghese came from a family in South India that was wealthy enough to educate daughters as well as sons. When the time came for her to decide what she wanted to do with her life, Mary chose to study medicine.

'I don't know how you can do that,' one of her school friends said. 'You have to clean dirty wounds, and you might even have to work with people with leprosy.'

'I certainly won't be doing that,' insisted Mary. 'But there are lots of other kinds of medicine.'

'Where do you want to study?' asked her companion.

'I want to go to Vellore, to the Christian hospital there that was founded in 1918 by a woman called Dr Ida Scudder.'

It was in 1946, when she was twenty-one years old, that Mary was accepted to train as a doctor at Vellore. She was thrilled ... and very scared. Dr Ida was, by then, an elderly lady. But the students saw her nearly every day and she prayed for them all individually. Mary loved listening to Dr Ida praying, for she seemed to be speaking to her very best friend.

1947 was a momentous year for India. That was when the land gained its freedom from Britain and began to govern itself. It was like a birth for the people of India and the rejoicing was tremendous. And there was another kind of birth too, for when Mary Verghese was a student she was born again, just as Jesus said we need to be to go to heaven. Mary Verghese became a Christian. Her family saw a difference when she went home to visit them.

'Pakavum! Adukkallai!' she heard the old cries once again. She strode to the gate and opened it.

'Joseph,' she said kindly. 'Someone will bring you food. But let me see your hands.'

The man held out his leprous hands in amazement.

'You need to go to the hospital,' Mary told him. 'The doctors there could help you.'

The following January it looked as though doctors would not be able to help Mary Verghese.

'Poor Mary,' her friend said. 'She went out on a drive with a crowd of students and the station wagon went off the road. Mary's terribly injured.'

'How terribly?'

'She may never walk again ... and her face has been slashed from her cheekbone to her chin.'

The two students stood in silence. There were no word to express the grief they felt.

The months that followed were awful for Mary. It was summer and the temperature soared. Her injuries were so serious that she was strapped into a plastic brace and perspex jacket. She felt as though she was cooking.

'Can you feel that?' nurses and doctors asked over and over again as they pricked her legs.

'Feel what?' Mary replied, not realising what they were doing.

'Am I ever going to walk?' she asked one day. That question took every ounce of her courage, for she already knew the answer. Her worst fears were true.

'I'm praying for you,' Dr Ida assured her. 'God hears and answers your prayers too.'

'But I'm never going to walk,' wept Mary. 'I'm never going to be a doctor.'

Dr Ida's eyes filled with compassion. 'You may not walk, my child. But don't rule out being a doctor.'

On black days Mary ruled it out totally. Her life was finished! But over the long months God helped her to begin to see just a tiny chink of light at the end of the tunnel.

'Mary,' said Dr Brand, when he called into her room one day. 'I think it's time you began thinking about your future.'

'I think about it all the time,' said Mary wearily.

'I mean your career as a doctor.'

'You must be joking,' the young woman snapped. 'That's over!'

'Why? Another few months and you'll be in a wheelchair. You have good arms and splendid surgeon's fingers. Your mind is the same as it was before.'

When Dr Brand left the room, Mary had to pinch herself to make sure she was awake.

Dr Paul Brand was a famous surgeon, and his speciality was operating on patients who were deformed because of leprosy. His encouragement and help led Mary to have hope for the future. Eventually she began seeing patients in the leprosy clinic. A month later Dr Brand had a surprising suggestion to make.

'Your best subject was surgery, Mary. What about it?'

His friend looked astounded. 'I'm a paraplegic.' (Paraplegic means Mary was unable to use her legs.)

'You don't operate with your feet,' Dr Brand said. 'Now, tomorrow I'm going to perform a hand operation and I want you to help me. Will you do that?'

It's hard to imagine all the feelings and thoughts that must have gone through that young woman's heart and mind before she smiled and said, rather shakily, 'I would like to very much.'

Dr Mary Verghese proved to be a splendid surgeon. It was not at all easy operating when sitting in a wheelchair, but she found new ways of doing things. She discovered that God's word is true, that with him all things are possible.

'Good afternoon, Mr Achamma,' she said, as her patient came in on crutches. 'Please sit down.'

The man sat down grumpily.

'Now, let me see your hands.'

Mary examined his damaged hands, and thought of the long ago time when she would have been terrified to touch someone with leprosy. 'I think we can help you. You may even be able to work again.'

'It's all right for you,' Mr Achamma complained. 'You don't know what it's like to have people looking at you and pointing at you all the time. It's horrible.'

Wheeling her chair round from behind her desk, Mary pulled it to a stop beside the man.

'I do,' she said. 'Yes, I do.'

'What a difference it makes having Mary in the department,' Dr Brand told a visitor. 'The patients can see how she copes with her difficulties and that inspires them to cope with their problems too.'

It was not always easy and there were times when it was terribly hard. Mary suffered a great deal of pain, especially in hot weather. But she knew God was with her, even in the hardest times. She met each new challenge head on. It took years, but Mary eventually learned to walk with braces on her legs, though she still often used a wheelchair. Towards the end of her life she was bed-ridden, but even then she inspired people.

'You went to America!' an amazed visitor exclaimed, looking at the elderly lady propped against her pillows.

'Yes,' smiled Mary. 'I studied at the Institute of Physical Medicine and Rehabilitation in New York. In fact, rehabilitation – helping people to make the most of what they are able to do – became my life's work. That's why I helped set up the Rehabilitation Department here at Vellore twenty years ago, in 1966. There was a day when I never thought I would be able to work, but I've had a wonderful life as a doctor. I've seen so many patients who thought their useful lives had ended – people damaged by, for example, accidents, tuberculosis, cancer, cerebral palsy – and I've seen them go on to do very worthwhile things.'

'And I hear you won the World Vision Award,' said the visitor.

'My work, and the work of many others, gained that award,' Mary said. 'And the money is being used to add to the rehabilitation block.'

Dr Mary Verghese did not see the building work completed. She died and went home to heaven in December 1986. Six years later her family donated money to build a little chapel on to the department. They knew that Mary's strength came from the Lord Jesus and they wanted to encourage others who were disabled to look to him for their help and their strength.

FACT FILE
Dr. Ida Scudder
Dr Ida Scudder was a medical missionary to India and the founder of the Vellore Christian Medical Centre. After graduating, she received a grant of $10,000 and opened a medical dispensary and hospital in Vellore. In 1918 she opened a medical school for women. Then in 1945 the college was opened to men as well as women. In 2003 the Vellore Christian Medical Centre hospital was the largest Christian hospital in the world, with 2000 beds. Its medical school was one of the premier medical colleges in India.

Keynote: Mary Verghese discovered that God's Word is true, that with him all things are possible. It is amazing that she managed to do all that she did from a wheelchair. But it is good to know that God can use us despite our problems and failures. Patients saw how Mary coped and it inspired them.

Think: As a child Mary didn't like to see ugly things. However, her mother told her that horrible things happen and that we have to face up to them. Think about this: when bad things happen we don't have to face up to them alone. God not only gives us the gift of other Christians to befriend us, God is with us himself. Jesus has promised that he will never leave us or forsake us. Sometimes human friends do leave us and we cannot always rely on people but we can always rely on God.

Prayer: Thank you, God, for the strengths and abilities that you have given me. Thank you for the strength and inspiration that Mary Verghese was to her patients. Even as she struggled she showed people your strength. Help me to show you to others in the way I live my life.

Maureen McKenna

Nine-year-old Maureen pushed the toes of her wellington boots into the shallow cracks in the stone wall and pulled herself up until she could just see over the top without being seen from the other side.

'Come on, Jean,' she whispered. 'There's nobody there.'

Jean and her friend scrambled on to the top of the wall and slid down the other side. They were as agile as cats and just as quick. Dodging between the shrubs, they crept into their favourite place in the doctor's garden. The sun shone down on them and the oak tree screened them from the back windows of the house. A rope swing hung from a branch on the tree, but the girls knew from past experience that it was best to wait a while in case anyone was at home who might come out into the garden and catch them.

Closing her eyes against the sun, Maureen wondered what it would be like to live in a fine house like this rather than in Glasgow's McAslin Street.

'When I grow up, I'll have a great big house with a garden,' she told Jean. 'I'm going to have clothes like the American film stars. I'll have my hair long enough that I can sit on it, and I'll have a refrigerator in the kitchen and a carpet on the kitchen floor.'

Jean giggled. 'Who do you think you are? Elvis Presley or Marilyn Monroe? I don't think they'll even have carpets on their kitchen floors. Imagine the mess it would get into when you were scrubbing your clothes on the washing board.'

Maureen thought of her mother up to her elbows in soapsuds, rubbing the dirty clothes up and down the corrugated washing board to clean them.

'Actually,' she said, in her very grandest voice, 'I'll have a maid to do my washing.'

'And I'll have wings and fly,' giggled Jean.

Dreams cost nothing, and Maureen could dream as much as she liked. Anything that cost money was different, for there wasn't much money around McAslin Street. At least, much of what there was found its way into the local public houses rather than the women's purses.

'Look,' Maureen said to her brother, half-way through a Friday evening. 'There's Mr Kelly staggering up the street again as usual. You'll never catch me drunk like that. Imagine him drinking his wages away when his two girls don't have shoes to wear.'

'You don't have shoes either,' her brother pointed out.

Maureen looked at him fiercely. 'But at least I've got wellington boots to keep my feet dry.'

Maureen had the marks on her legs to prove it. Because she wore wellington boots all winter, she had red raw rings around her legs where they rubbed when she walked.

'When I'm grown up,' she laughed aloud, 'I'll walk through puddles wearing such high heeled shoes that my feet won't get the least bit wet.'

Maureen's mother looked at her and smiled.

'What a dreamer you are,' she said. 'I hope your dreams come true.'

Before many years had passed, one of Maureen's dreams looked as if it might come true. She dreamed of swimming for Scotland and she was heading in the right direction.

'How did you get the money for the swimming pool?' Jean asked her friend, as Maureen went to the Townhead Baths for the second time in a week.

'I got a penny from Mrs Murphy for scrubbing her kitchen floor, and three pence for a lemonade bottle at the shop.'

'Where did you find the lemonade bottle?' demanded Jean, who would have liked three pence herself.

'That's my secret,' Maureen said, winking at her friend. 'Let's just say that there's a certain man who is sometimes so drunk that he puts glass bottles in the bin rather than getting three pence back on them. And I know which is his dustbin.'

'I'd like you to go for trials with a view to swimming for the South West of Scotland team,' Miss Wolfe, her gym teacher, said.

Maureen ran home as though her feet had wings. But it wasn't all good news, for it meant a new swimming costume. Although Mr McKenna thought his daughter was wasting her time swimming, his wife scrimped and saved for a swimming costume. Maureen could not have been happier if she'd been given a golden silk ball-gown.

'Remember to go to the doctor,' Mrs McKenna said, as Maureen left for school.

'I'll remember,' called the girl. 'But he's useless. I can't hear very well, and he doesn't help. It's a waste of time going.'

But that afternoon, when she was at the Ear, Nose and Throat Clinic, Maureen McKenna's world fell apart.

'I know you're keen on swimming,' the doctor said. 'But the pressure under the water is making your hearing worse. You'll have to choose between swimming and hearing.'

Whatever he said after that was completely lost on Maureen for she was screaming inside herself. And each silent scream yelled out that life isn't fair. 'It just isn't fair!'

It was not that Maureen's father was unkind, it was just that he didn't know what to say when he heard the news.

'No, it's not fair,' he agreed. 'But so what? That's life.'

Because Maureen was a clever girl, she was selected to go to a different school from her friends in McAslin Street. That meant she was different from her friends, and she felt different from her new school friends too. Some of them had refrigerators in their kitchens and a number of her new friends had piano lessons after school. Others did country dancing. Maureen was different. Her after-school activity was scrubbing the communal staircases in several of the closes in McAslin Street.

'Walking back to happiness,' she sang, as she scrubbed.

Some of the women on the stair joined in the pop song, for Maureen had a fine voice and could be heard in the flats.

'How can you sing when you're scrubbing stairs?' Jean asked. 'I'd grump my way up every step.'

Maureen grinned. 'I love the job,' she said. 'I start at the bottom and scrub my way up dozens of steps till I reach the light of the roof window at the top. I feel as though I'm climbing a ladder to heaven. And I get paid for the pleasure.'

'Fine chance you have of going to heaven,' Jean laughed.

Not long afterwards the McKennas had a visitor.

'God bless you,' he said, as he left. 'God is good.'

'I don't believe that any more,' Maureen snapped. 'Because every time something good happens to me, it's just snatched away.'

'A bus driver?' thought Maureen, when she saw the advertisement some years later. 'I'd like to be a bus driver. That would turn a few heads, for I don't think I've ever seen a woman at the wheel of a double-decker bus.'

Maureen went through the training and, much to her passengers' amazement, began driving a bus.

'Look! It's a woman at the wheel!' children shouted, as she drove past.

'I don't like the look of that,' said an elderly man, as he took his life in his hands and climbed on the bus.

'You're just old fashioned,' his wife told him. 'A woman will be as good as a man if she gets us home with the shopping.'

Sadly Maureen's life did not go 'happily ever after'. Having started to drink in the early 1960s, when she was in her mid-teens, she took up with a man who also drank, and who was bad to her. They moved from place to place and job to job, but their situation went from bad to desperate. Maureen often went back to her mum, bruised and broken-hearted. Each time she used alcohol to drown her sorrows. After a particularly bad spell, she went to a meeting of Alcoholics Anonymous, hoping to find help. There she met a recovering alcoholic named Hugh McKenna – though they were both McKennas they were not related. Hugh was a Christian, and the Lord had helped him to come off drink and stay clear of it. He told Maureen that he had a friend who could help her, and his name was Jesus. After more troubled times Maureen became a Christian, and some years later she and Hugh were married. They loved each other very much indeed, and they both loved the Lord Jesus Christ.

'Tell me about Hugh's job,' someone asked Maureen, soon after they were married. 'He seems to work very strange hours.'

'He works the hours he's needed,' Maureen answered. 'You see, Hugh's job is to go down into the city centre late at night to help people in need.'

'What kind of people?'

143

'Many are drug addicts,' Maureen explained, 'some of them just young teenagers. Then there are the homeless people, and other poor sad souls out on the streets at all hours.'

'And what does Hugh do?'

Maureen thought about her husband's work as she replied. 'He takes them soup, tea and sandwiches. And he listens to their problems and worries.'

'He must hear some terrible things.'

'Yes,' said Maureen. 'And so do I.'

'What do you mean? Are you out at night with Hugh?'

'Some nights,' said Maureen. 'You see, sometimes he meets young women on the streets, and it's better if I'm there.'

'But what about Paul?'

Maureen smiled at the thought of her little boy.

'Mum looks after him while I'm out with Hugh. He's asleep in his bed anyway.'

'I don't know how you can do that,' her friend commented, shaking her head.

'We do it because we believe that's what God wants us to do,' Maureen said. 'And you'd be surprised at how often we're able to tell the people we meet about the Lord Jesus.'

Maureen became more and more involved in the work in the centre of Glasgow. She and Hugh were well known by some of the most needy people in the city, from young children being brought up in poverty and teenagers addicted to drink and drugs, through to mothers struggling to made ends meet, and old men and women who had nowhere to call their home. Eventually, in 1998, they founded Open Door Trust Glasgow, a charity dedicated to the work they were doing.

Jackie Ross, who lived in the North of Scotland, knew about the work Hugh and Maureen were doing. For years Mr Ross had been involved in work with Blythswood Trust, which also helped poor and needy people, both in the UK and abroad. Blythswood helped supply Open Door Trust with clothes and other things that they needed for the people they met. Mr Ross invited the McKennas and a friend to travel north to visit Blythswood's depot.

'Could you make use of an old double-decker bus?' Mr Ross asked his visitors.

'Look at this!' exclaimed Hugh, as they climbed the stair of the bus. 'The downstairs is equipped with a cooker, fridge, sink, tables and chairs. There's even a children's playroom there. And the upstairs would be ideal for talking to people in private.'

'Could we use it?' whistled Maureen. 'We most certainly could! We could go out in it for our city centre night patrol. It would be ideal for serving our snacks, for sheltering the mothers and children we sometimes meet, when they've been thrown out of their homes. Then there's people who just want to talk. They could meet with us upstairs.'

'The only problem is that you'd need someone with a Public Service Vehicle Licence to drive it,' admitted Mr Ross. 'And it would take time for that person to do his training.'

Maureen grinned from ear to ear.

'That person would be a her rather than a him, and it would be me,' Maureen laughed. 'I used to be a bus driver.'

Hugh just loved the expression on Mr Ross's face.

The Big White Bus was serviced, cleaned and had its name painted on the side, before being delivered to Glasgow. With Maureen in the driver's seat, Open Door Trust Glasgow reached out and helped those the Lord took them to. People came on board for soup and friendship, for sandwiches and advice, for tea and shelter, for support and safety. And some, who came on board looking for a friend, discovered that the best friend of all is Jesus.

'We'll never run out of work,' Maureen said, early in 2000. 'Last year there were 104 drug-related deaths in and around Glasgow.'

'That was last year's bad news,' said Hugh. 'But remember the good news. Remember the day we took twenty-five city children to visit a farm and gave them the day of their lives.'

'And remember buying them each a pair of shoes on the way home,' added Maureen. 'They were so pleased with them.'

Maureen smiled, and thought back to the days when her only footwear was wellington boots that rubbed a red ring round her legs.

'And wasn't Christmas wonderful?' Hugh remembered. 'God used Open Door Trust Glasgow to make so many children happy, children for whom Christmas would not have been special otherwise.'

'Think what we can do in the future,' said Maureen.

Even though she was in her mid-fifties she still had dreams, just as she had had as a child.

But God had other plans. At Easter 2002 Maureen McKenna died after a short illness. Having worked with many people who were distressed, who were hurting, who were dying, God took her home to heaven where there is no sadness, no pain and no death. The work of Open Door Trust, Glasgow, still continues today with the help of many others who have the same love for Jesus and humanity that Maureen had.

FACT FILE
Glasgow
Glasgow has a population of around 600,000. It is Scotland's largest city and commercial capital. It is the U.K.'s largest retail centre after London. The motto of Glasgow used to be, 'Let Glasgow Flourish through the preaching of his Word and the praising of his name.' This reflects Glasgow's strong Christian past.

Keynote: Maureen McKenna had quite a struggle with alcoholism. She made mistakes but in the end she sought help. She met Hugh but more importantly she came to love Jesus Christ. God used her to reach out to others who struggled with life, drug abuse and homelessness. We all make mistakes and failure is difficult to come to terms with. In Psalm 77 David realised something amazing about God. 'You are the God who performs miracles; you display your power among the peoples.' God can display his power in your life by taking your mistakes and disasters and making something good out of them. He can change you. Jesus Christ can be your Saviour. People will see your life and realise how great God is.

Think: Maureen's life saw hardship, disappointment, mistakes, failure and success. We should realise that all these things are part of life. We need to face up to disappointment and success and there can be problems with both. If you have disappointment in life, don't dwell on it and get bitter. Take your trouble to God. If you have success, don't dwell on that either. Thank God for giving you strengths and abilities to be successful.

 Prayer: Dear Lord, thank you for my life and help me to make the most of it. When things go wrong or when things go well you are with me. Help me to work for you and to study your Word so that I will know the truth and be able to teach the truth to others. Help me to pray to you regularly so that I can know you and bring others to you.

Quiz

How much can you remember about the ten girls who used their talents? Try answering these questions to find out.

Anne Lawson

1. What was the name of the girl martyred in Wigton?
2. What did Anne study at university?
3. What mission did Anne work for?

Selina, Countess of Huntingdon

1. How much money did Selina's father inherit?
2. What did Selina inherit from her grandfather?
3. What were the names of the three preachers Selina heard during the 1700s?

Mildred Cable

1. What did the missionary have on her collar?
2. What desert did Mildred travel through?
3. What is the name of the trade route through that desert?

Katie Ann Mackinnon

1. What did Katie Ann decide to be when she was ten years old?
2. What country did Katie Ann go to in 1971?
3. How many children's homes did Katie Ann leave when she retired to Scotland?

Sarah Edwards

1. How old was Sarah when her father died?
2. Who did Sarah marry?
3. To what people did Sarah's husband go as a missionary in 1751?

Patricia St John

1. What country did Patricia's father work in?
2. What country in Africa did Patricia go to?
3. What was the name of the book Patricia wrote about Onesimus?

Helen Roseveare

1. What did Helen and her sister see in the skies above Kent during the 2nd World War?
2. What happened to Helen when she went to a house party instead of going home at Christmas?
3. What was Helen's nickname in the Congo?

Harriet Beecher Stowe

1. What awful sight did Harriet witness in Cincinnati?
2. What was the name of the weekly paper that published Harriet's anti-slavery story?
3. What was the name of the book when it was published?

Mary Verghese

1. What disease did Joseph suffer from in the story?
2. What happened to Mary which meant that she had to use a wheel-chair?
3. What award did Mary win for her work?

Maureen McKenna

1. What sport did Maureen enjoy as a young girl?
2. What city did she work in?
3. What surprising skill did Maureen learn which helped her help the homeless?

How well did you do?

Go to the opposite page to find out.

Quiz Answers

1. Margaret.
2. Zoology.
3. M.A.F. (Mission Aviation Fellowship).
4. £20.
5. His temper.
6. John Wesley, Charles Wesley, George Whitefield.
7. An embroidered Bible verse.
8. Gobi Desert.
9. The Silk Road.
10. A nurse.
11. Kenya.
12. Three.
13. Four years old.
14. Jonathan Edwards.
15. Native American Indians.
16. Brazil.
17. Morocco.
18. *Twice Freed.*
19. British and German bombers.
20. She became a Christian.
21. Mama Luka.
22. A slave auction where a husband and wife were separated.
23. *The National Era.*
24. *Uncle Tom's Cabin.*
25. Leprosy.
26. A car accident.
27. The World Vision Award.
28. Swimming.
29. Glasgow.
30. She learnt to be a bus driver.

Ten Girls who Made a Difference:
ISBN 978-1-85792-776-4
Monica of Thagaste, Catherine Luther,
Susanna Wesley, Ann Judson, Maria Taylor,
Susannah Spurgeon, Bethan Lloyd-Jones,
Edith Schaeffer, Sabina Wurmbrand,
Ruth Bell Graham.

Ten Boys who Made History:
ISBN 978-1-85792-836-5
Charles Spurgeon, Jonathan Edwards,
Samuel Rutherford, D L Moody,
Martin Lloyd Jones, A W Tozer, John Owen, Robert Murray
McCheyne, Billy Sunday,
George Whitfield.

Ten Girls who Made History:
ISBN 978-1-85792-837-2
Ida Scudder, Betty Green, Jeanette Li,
Mary Jane Kinnaird, Bessie Adams,
Emma Dryer, Lottie Moon, Florence Nightingale, Henrietta
Mears, Elisabeth Elliot.

Ten Boys who Didn't Give In:
ISBN 978-1-84550-035-1
Polycarp, Alban, Sir John Oldcastle
Thomas Cramer, George Wishart,
James Chalmers, Dietrich Bonhoeffer
Nate Saint, Ivan Moiseyev
Graham Staines

Ten Girls who Didn't Give In:
ISBN 978-1-84550-036-8
Blandina, Perpetua, Lady Jane Grey,
Anne Askew, Lysken Dirks, Marion Harvey,
Margaret Wilson, Judith Weinberg,
Betty Stam, Esther John

CHRISTIAN FOCUS PUBLICATIONS

Christian Focus | Christian Heritage | CF4K | Mentor

Christian Focus Publications publishes books for adults and children under its four main imprints: Christian Focus, CF4K, Mentor and Christian Heritage. Our books reflect our conviction that God's Word is reliable and Jesus is the way to know him, and live for ever with him.

Our children's publication list covers pre-school to early teens. We also publish personal and family devotional titles, biographies and inspirational stories that children will love.

From pre-school board books to teenage apologetics, we have it covered!

Christian Focus Publications Ltd,
Geanies House, Fearn, Ross-shire,
IV20 1TW, Scotland,
United Kingdom.
www.christianfocus.com

CF4•K
Because you're never
too young to know Jesus

Author Information:
Irene Howat

Irene Howat is an award-winning author and poet who lives in Scotland. She has published many biographical books for all ages and is particularly well-known for her biographical material. She has written many books about the lives of different Christians from around the world. She has also written an autobiographical work entitled: *Pain My Companion*.

Start collecting this series now!

Ten Boys who used their Talents:
ISBN 978-1-84550-146-4

Paul Brand, Ghillean Prance, C.S.Lewis,
C.T. Studd, Wilfred Grenfell, J.S. Bach,
James Clerk Maxwell, Samuel Morse,
George Washington Carver, John Bunyan.

Ten Girls who used their Talents:
ISBN 978-1-84550-147-1

Helen Roseveare, Maureen McKenna,
Anne Lawson, Harriet Beecher Stowe,
Sarah Edwards, Selina Countess of Huntingdon, Mildred Cable,
Katie Ann MacKinnon,
Patricia St. John, Mary Verghese.

Ten Boys who Changed the World:
ISBN 978-1-85792-579-1

David Livingstone, Billy Graham, Brother Andrew,
John Newton, William Carey, George Müller,
Nicky Cruz, Eric Liddell, Luis Palau,
Adoniram Judson.

Ten Girls who Changed the World:
ISBN 978-1-85792-649-1

Corrie Ten Boom, Mary Slessor,
Joni Eareckson Tada, Isobel Kuhn,
Amy Carmichael, Elizabeth Fry, Evelyn Brand, Gladys Aylward,
Catherine Booth, Jackie Pullinger.

Ten Boys who Made a Difference:
ISBN 978-1-85792-775-7

Augustine of Hippo, Jan Hus, Martin Luther,
Ulrich Zwingli, William Tyndale, Hugh Latimer,
John Calvin, John Knox, Lord Shaftesbury,
Thomas Chalmers.